OPPORTUNITIES

in

Chiropractic Careers

REVISED EDITION

I0702315

BART N. GREEN, D.C., M.S.ED.
CLAIRE JOHNSON, D.C., M.S.ED.
LOUIS SPORTELLI, D.C.

VGM Career Books

Chicago   New York   San Francisco   Lisbon   London   Madrid   Mexico City
Milan   New Delhi   San Juan   Seoul   Singapore   Sydney   Toronto

The *McGraw·Hill* Companies

Library of Congress Cataloging-in-Publication Data

Green, Bart N.
      Opportunities in chiropractic careers / Bart N. Green, Claire Johnson,
Louis Sportelli. — Rev. ed. Previous ed. published under : Schafer, R. C.
         p.   cm. (VGM opportunities series)
      ISBN 0-07-141164-X
      1. Chiropractic—Vocational guidance.   I. Johnson, Claire.
II. Sportelli, Louis.   III. Title.   IV. Series.

RZ236.S32   2004
615.5'34'023—dc22   2003025807

*This book is dedicated to Richard C. Schafer, D.C. Dr. Schafer's
distinguished career was marked by his numerous book publications,
including the 1987 and 1993 editions of* Opportunities in Chiropractic
Careers. *These books were, and continue to be, used by thousands of
chiropractic students worldwide. We are grateful for his unwavering
dedication to the chiropractic profession and are honored to keep
his work alive as a new team of authors.*

1 2 3 4 5 6 7 8 9 0   LBM/LBM   3 2 1 0 9 8 7 6 5 4

ISBN 0-07-141164-X

Interior design by Rattray Design

McGraw-Hill books are available at special quantity discounts to use as premiums and
sales promotions, or for use in corporate training programs. For more information,
please write to the Director of Special Sales, Professional Publishing, McGraw-Hill, Two
Penn Plaza, New York, NY 10121-2298. Or contact your local bookstore.

The views expressed in this publication are those of the authors and do not reflect the
official policy or position of the Department of the Navy, Department of Defense, or the
United States Government.

CONTENTS

Foreword   vii

Preface   xv

1. Overview of the Chiropractic Profession   1

Chiropractic in the health-care system. Chiropractic patients. Chiropractic approach to health.

2. History of Chiropractic   15

Early health care in America. The birth of chiropractic. Did chiropractors invent spinal manipulation? Contributions of early civilizations to health care. Chiropractic pioneers. Licensing. Development of educational standards.

3. Chiropractic as a Professional Career   35

Professional and economic rewards. What are the
career opportunities? Women and minorities in
chiropractic. Chiropractic abroad. Chiropractic
outreach programs.

4. A Day in the Life of a Chiropractor   53

Typical workday. Patient care. Work conditions.
Personal attributes. Conditions treated. Wellness.
Duties outside of the practice. Visiting a chiropractor.

5. Educational Preparation for Chiropractic College   75

Admissions. Selecting a chiropractic college.
Chiropractic colleges in North America.

6. The Chiropractic College Experience   89

Profile of a typical chiropractic student. Student
orientation. Curriculum. Academic standing and
grading. Student services. The National Board of
Chiropractic Examiners. Professional degree and
licensure requirements. Continuing education.

7. Financing a Chiropractic Education   107

Costs. Student scholarships. Student financial aid.
Part-time employment.

Appendix A: Chiropractic Organizations
   and Websites   115
Appendix B: Doctor of Chiropractic Programs   119
Appendix C: State Boards of Chiropractic
   Examiners   127
Bibliography   137

FOREWORD

My own life experiences have occurred in a parallel with the chiropractic profession. My father, brother, sister, nephew, and daughter are doctors of chiropractic, as are numerous other cousins and members of the extended family tree.

When I chose the legal profession for my life's work, I had few thoughts that my path would cross that of the chiropractic profession. As it turned out, my work has frequently been involved with chiropractic, primarily through engagements designed to ward off overzealous competitors not focused on the well-being of patients. I was privileged to be the lead trial counsel for what turned out to be sixteen years (1976–92) of successful antitrust litigation designed to stop medical trade associations from conspiring to eliminate the rapidly growing and competitive profession of chiropractic (*Wilk et al. v. AMA et al.*).

Growing up during the late 1930s through early 1950s in a chiropractic family, I remember the constant admonitions: eat balanced meals; do not overeat; excess sun causes cancer; keep covered up (the five boys in our family played in the park with sombrero-like hats); sleep before midnight is extremely useful sleep; use vitamin supplements if your diet is not balanced; brush your teeth at least twice a day; make sure your walking gait is uniform, or try to find out why it is not and correct it; keep your shoulders back and breathe deeply; don't lift excessive weight; drink plenty of water; sit upright; bathe frequently; don't inhale dust or chemicals; don't smoke; if you have to drink, be moderate; avoid pharmaceuticals unless absolutely essential; and so on.

My father adjusted me and my siblings on a regular basis. I'm sixty-eight years old now, and my only health complaint is a head cold every two or three years—and my children tell me I should watch my weight. I have no joint or muscle pain. I sleep seven to eight hours each night, and I tell my young partners and associates (possibly to their consternation) that I hope to go on a three-day workweek when I am ninety. I seem to be in the 5.65th percentile mentioned in the 1995 RAND study, which is quoted later. My experience may not be all that unusual.

There is a well-known adage: When something is new, and you didn't think of it, condemn it; when it looks promising, try to copy its best features; when it succeeds beyond all expectations, claim that you invented it. That is a perfect description of what has happened to chiropractic from 1895 through the year 2003. The dominant medical world condemned the profession for eighty-five years; then sound research, often to the complete surprise of highly disciplined and ethical medical researchers, demonstrated the clear superiority of much of what chiropractic has to offer. Subsequently the medical profession announced that it was intrigued by nutrition, exercise, lifestyle, and care of the body's neuromusculoskeletal system. Now that chiropractic education, training, and service to humankind have witnessed a massive shift in whole segments of the health-care paradigm, and the transfer of millions of patients and significant amounts of health-care dollars to chiropractic care and advice, one sees many medical schools rearranging their curricula to include many components of chiropractic and claiming it was theirs all along. How ironic!

After watching the opponents of chiropractic try to explain away startling evidence of the superiority of chiropractic care versus medical care as reported in workmen's compensation surveys, I was most pleased to hear a Ph.D. economist, retained by the defendants in the *Wilk v. AMA* case, admit to the judge: "Even the defendants' economic witness, Mr. Lynk (a Ph.D.), assumed that chiropractors outperformed medical physicians in the treatment of certain conditions and he believed that was a reasonable assumption."

How refreshing: it is hard to put a negative slant on an honest economist's conclusions using the mathematics of hard reality.

In 1974, some eight million Americans sought the services of doctors of chiropractic. This number, as of 2003, had grown dramatically to thirty million. More than ninety million Americans have sought chiropractic services at some point in their lives. More chiropractors are needed in light of the fact that sooner rather than later, most of the remaining 180 million Americans will come to seek their services.

A study undertaken by the RAND Corporation, which initially was not directed toward chiropractic in any way, is almost startling in what it discovered. RAND tracks groups of various citizens to follow their living and health habits. These are called Comprehensive Geriatric Assessment (CGAs) groups. One of the groups was of people seventy-five years of age. The group consisted of 414 members. One day, while reviewing one of the groups, it was noticed that twenty-three (5.65 percent) members used the services of chiropractic. "Chiropractic users were less likely to have been hospitalized, less likely to have used a nursing home, more likely to report better health status, more likely to be mobile in the community. They were less likely to use prescription drugs."

Yes, it is possible that the twenty-three could have been helped in their healthy status by being under the care of doctors of chiropractic. On the other hand, they could have sought the services of chiropractors because they were already healthier and more active and, because of this, understood how they could benefit by being under such care.

In either case, it has become increasingly and dramatically well known that the chiropractic profession is the leader in matters pertaining to "wellness." As this awareness has grown, it has become clear that any perception of doctors of chiropractic as only addressing spinal problems is incorrect. Of course, it is true that they have great knowledge, based on their superior education in the field of the musculoskeletal system, and that spinal health is one of the outstanding contributions they make to health care. In addition, however, they also have highly trained expertise in the field of wellness care, advising their patients on how to pursue a healthier lifestyle so that constant and/or regular sickness does not assail them. These citizens are made far more alert to how they should live their lives so as to avoid the downfalls of our culture in the area of health. The "old" way of doing things—going to the doctor and, in effect, saying, "Here is my body, doctor; I got it sick, you get it well"—is a very poor orientation and one that clearly leads a person into the trap of ill health.

In May 2000, *Consumer Reports* reported the results of a survey of forty-six thousand people, showing that, for back pain, the sixteen thousand (35 percent) who used alternative therapies more often chose chiropractic care over all other kinds of care for related disorders. Chiropractic received more positive responses ("Helped me feel much better") than any other form of care including prescription drugs and over-the-counter drugs. This is significant because 32.2 percent of persons ages eighteen to twenty-nine, 41.5 percent of those between thirty and forty-four, 49.2 percent of those between forty-five and fifty-nine, 43.7 percent of those over sixty, and 41.7 percent of our overall population suffer from back pain, with the majority of these being women.

Additionally, information concerning "patient satisfaction" is dramatic. Research conducted throughout the world, much of which was relied on by the federal government for its 1994 guidelines published by the Agency for Health Care Policy and Research, shows that spinal manipulation for low-back pain is safe and effective for both pain management and improved functionality.

Here are excerpts from a few recent studies highlighting patient satisfaction with chiropractic care. *The Manga Report*, funded by the Ontario Ministry of Health in Canada, states: "For the management of low back pain, chiropractic care is the most effective treatment, and it should be fully integrated into the government's health care system." (Manga, et al.) This is further supported by a landmark study conducted in Great Britain: "Chiropractic treatment was more effective than hospital outpatient management, mainly for patients with chronic or severe back pain." (Meade) Further evidence of patient satisfaction can be summarized by the following report: "Chiropractic patients were three times more satisfied with their care than patients of family practice physicians." (Cherkin and MacCornack)

Chiropractic care for a variety of neuromusculoskeletal conditions is gaining wider acceptance among society. Medical referrals to doctors of chiropractic, particularly for back pain, are increasing rapidly. Approximately 89 percent of conditions cared for by chiropractors relate to the musculoskeletal system, which comprises 60 percent of the body's systems. Few will argue the positive benefits of chiropractic care for such conditions. For example, an article in *Spine Journal* (North American Spine Society) designated spinal manipulation as "Generally accepted, well-established and widely used." Additional support is seen in the following research: "A majority of family physicians (in the state of Washington) admitted to having encouraged patients to see a chiropractor, and two-thirds indicated a desire to learn more about what chiropractors do." (Curtis)

Chiropractors emphasize the importance of maintaining good health. If a person were to acquire a new automobile at age sixteen and was told that this was the only automobile he or she would ever have, we know how carefully he or she would care for that automobile. The person would have the oil changed when due, avoid potholes that could damage the suspension system, get the hinges on the doors lubricated regularly, wax the surfaces of the automobile, keep the wheels in alignment, use appropriate grades of gasoline, and more. To do otherwise, and to have to junk the car earlier than would have been necessary, would leave the individual without a car and with all the associated inconveniences for the rest of his or her life.

The same is true of the human body. We are given one body to use for the entirety of our lives. When we do not care for this "once in a lifetime" body by eating correctly, exercising regularly, taking care of its structural integrity, avoiding smoking and other excesses, and wearing seat belts, we know that our mortality will be challenged at a much younger age than the actuarial tables might predict. No amount of drugs or surgeries or other heroic measures to repair what often we ourselves have caused or allowed to happen through our lack of responsibility in caring for ourselves will adequately correct these ills.

I have watched those who have sought and received chiropractic care and advice follow a much healthier lifestyle. I have also watched how the problems they so often acquired with their musculoskeletal systems were corrected at an early or later stage of life so that the dynamics of those systems functioned in normal ways. No one else seems to be able to provide this highly educated and trained service. In my opinion, chiropractors deal with this complex system like no other provider group. Studies and facts consistently show this. Perhaps my undergraduate degree in mechanical engineering has helped me to better appreciate the chiropractor's approach to the structural mechanics of the human body.

As a patent/antitrust attorney, I am deeply involved in all elements of America's competitive economic markets. Health care is no different, and the chiropractic profession is among the leaders in this area. As an attorney, I have been able to influence dozens, perhaps hundreds, of my colleagues to seek chiropractic care. I am not surprised by how often those people take the time to thank me.

The future is bright for this profession, and that is why I am so very proud to have my daughter Mary hold the distinguished title of Doctor of Chiropractic.

George P. McAndrews, Esq.

PREFACE

THIS BOOK IS written for high school and college students who are considering a health-care profession as a career. The field of chiropractic is an exciting and rewarding health-care profession, and the authors' objectives are to provide an explanation of the field of chiropractic and the opportunities available within it.

Because the practice of chiropractic, as well as that of all health-care professions, is governed by statutes in each separate jurisdiction, the information offered in this book is general in nature.

Presented in brief form are an overview of the profession and career opportunities available in the chiropractic field. An in-depth look into the day of a chiropractor is provided for those who have never been to a chiropractor's office. Several chapters present information regarding the educational preparation necessary to enter chiropractic college, what it is like once you are there, and how to finance a chiropractic education. A brief history of chiropractic is also included.

The opportunities for doctors of chiropractic are greater today than ever before. Chiropractic offers both men and women an opportunity to serve the health and welfare of our nation and enjoy many personal advantages as well. Chiropractic offers the dedicated individual independence, prestige, excellent working conditions, a rewarding income, and a satisfying career.

1

Overview of the Chiropractic Profession

Chiropractic is one of the largest health-care professions in the United States and the fastest-growing primary health-care profession in the world. There are more than sixty-five thousand active licenses for doctors of chiropractic in the United States, and approximately eight thousand students are currently studying in accredited chiropractic educational programs. Doctors of Chiropractic (D.C.s) provide primary health care to an increasing number of patients each year. The D.C. is concerned with human health and disease processes, considers each patient as an integrated being, and gives special attention to spinal mechanics and the health status of a patient's nervous, muscular, and skeletal systems. Uniquely, chiropractors employ natural means to help their patients heal. Foremost among these methods are chiropractic adjustments. Typically, using their hands, D.C.s apply specific and controlled movements to the various joints of the body to help normalize its structure and function. With its rapidly expanding utilization and focus on conservative, natural care, chiropractic is a very exciting and rewarding career to consider.

Chiropractic in the Health-Care System

The United States federal government and all state legislatures recognize chiropractic doctors as portal-of-entry health-care providers. A portal-of-entry health-care provider is a doctor who is the first to see a patient who may be presenting with a particular complaint. As portal-of-entry doctors, D.C.s are trained to diagnose and manage a broad spectrum of health problems as well as provide preventive health care. In the United States, there are three healing arts licensed to provide such care; in order of both the numbers of practitioners and public utilization, they are the allopathic (traditional medicine), chiropractic, and osteopathic professions. As the second-largest portal-of-entry profession, chiropractors provide more than 190 million office visits annually to Americans, and approximately 4.5 million Canadians use the services of a chiropractor each year.

Factors common among all recognized healing arts include licensure in all states; educational standards that are maintained by an agency meeting the requirements of, and recognized by, the U.S. Department of Education; inclusion in state and federal health-care programs; and utilization of standardized diagnostic procedures. Although therapeutic approaches may differ, each healing art is based upon basic sciences such as anatomy, physiology, pathology, biochemistry, and others.

Chiropractic health care is provided in federal programs such as Medicare, Medicaid, the Government Employees Hospital Association Benefit Plan, the Mailhandlers' Benefit Plan, and the Postmasters' Benefit Plan, and is included in both the Railroad Retirement Act and the Longshoremen's and Harbor Workers' Compensation Act. Chiropractic students are qualified to receive federal student loan assistance, and D.C.s are authorized by the President of the United States to serve as commissioned health-care officers in the U.S. armed forces. On January 23, 2002, legislation was signed mandating the establishment of a permanent chiropractic benefit within the Department of Veterans Affairs health-care system (H.R. 3447). In 2000, a bill from the Department of Defense known as the National Defense Authorization Act was signed into law, which provides that military personnel have access to chiropractic care.

Chiropractors now serve as an important part of the health-care team in numerous armed services health-care facilities across the United States, including the prestigious Walter Reed Army Hospital in Washington, D.C., and the National Naval Medical Center in Bethesda, Maryland. In addition, chiropractic is included in the health insurance policies of virtually every major insurance carrier and in all state Workers' Compensation Acts. A substantial number of major international, national, and local unions (for example, railroad and rubber workers) and major industrial employers (for example, General Motors) provide for chiropractic services in their health and welfare plans for all their members and employees.

Chiropractic Patients

It is difficult to estimate the exact number of people receiving chiropractic care each year. A recent nationwide telephone survey estimated that approximately 11 percent of the American population, or approximately twenty-eight million people, seek chiropractic care in a given period of time, and this figure is growing. (Meeker and Haldeman, 2002) Chiropractors account for about 30 percent of all visits made to complementary and alternative practitioners. (Meeker and Haldeman, 2002)

Several surveys taken both within and without the profession have indicated that there is no measurable difference between chiropractic patients and those of any other healing art relative to age, sex, occupation, income status, education, or any other social factor.

Tens of millions of Americans choose to receive chiropractic services. About one out of every three Americans routinely selects alternative health care. Patients make chiropractic a regular part of their health-care program, even if personal out-of-pocket expense may be necessary. If there is one primary health-care profession that can point to private sector demand and to marketplace viability for economic validation, it is chiropractic. Thousands of consumers decide daily to invest their money for chiropractic services regardless if traditional medical care is available through insurance or government programs at a more subsidized cost or at no cost at all. Consumers make this choice because of the unique benefits chiropractic offers.

An article in the *Journal of the American Medical Association* affirmed that Americans recently made more visits to nonmedical providers (629 million visits) than to medical physicians (386 million visits). Expenditures associated with use of alternative therapy in 1997 amounted to approximately $27 billion. This figure is comparable to the $29.3 billion spent for all out-of-pocket medical physician services in the United States. (Eisenberg et al., 1998) Thus patients are making the choice to include other health-care methods, such as chiropractic, in meeting their health-care needs.

Chiropractic Approach to Health

The doctor of chiropractic is primarily concerned with the functioning and wellness of the body. Central to the philosophy of chiropractic is the idea that the body is a self-regulating organism capable of healing itself, provided that not too much damage has already been done. Chiropractors use their hands to correct dysfunctional areas of the spine and sometimes other parts of the body, which chiropractors call "chiropractic subluxations." Because of the relationship between the body's structure and function, chiropractic subluxations are thought to stimulate neural reflexes mediated in the spine and nervous system that can cause disturbances of body functions that stimulate, produce, or mimic various disorders. Other words used for the term chiropractic subluxation include "joint dysfunction" and "vertebral subluxation complex."

Structure and Function in Health and Disease

The relationship between human structure (anatomy) and function (physiology) has always been a primary focus of chiropractic. While it is common knowledge that a diseased organ may cause symptoms to appear in distant parts of the body, chiropractors have long suspected that neurological disturbances in the spinal column and other areas may cause symptoms and dysfunction to appear in remote organs and tissues. The body is integrally related; the nervous system has a significant impact on all functions of the body.

Balancing and harmonizing body systems are thought to result in normal function. Many chiropractors approach the patient as a total being in relation to her or his environment, rather than looking at the body from a purely chemical or organic viewpoint. A comprehensive health-care system is considered to be more than an attempt to merely suppress symptoms by giving medicine or removing diseased organs by surgery. Many diseases defy successful treatment by surgery or medical therapy alone. Although medicine or surgery may be necessary in some cases, the reason that an organ failed to function normally in the first place is often unclear. The suppression of symptoms or the removal of diseased tissue or organs often cannot guarantee the patient's return to optimal health. Chiropractic doctors believe that a comprehensive health-care system must be a great deal more than just the removal of symptoms, but a focus on total health.

Because of their interest in the relationship between the spine and nervous system and their expertise in managing such problems, chiropractors are sometimes viewed by the public as being only back and neck pain doctors. However, many patients seek chiropractic care to learn how to promote and maintain their health, and some seek relief from other problems related to headache, sports injuries, and nonmusculoskeletal disorders. Scientific investigations of the value of chiropractic care for such conditions are ongoing.

The Holistic Approach of Chiropractic

Holism is the theory that the determining factors in nature as a whole are greater than the sum of their parts. (Coulter, 1999) The human body is still a mystery, even after we add up all the tissues, organs, and systems in the laboratory. Chiropractors recognize this in their approach to health care.

Our skeletal structure is more than a bony cage to hold our vital organs or a bony rack on which nature has attached our muscles. We are more than an assortment of independent organs or a maze of parts. The unifying, coordinating, and controlling forces within our bodies are essentially the nervous, hormonal, and circulatory systems. There is no organ, tissue, or cell of the body that is not influenced in some way directly or indirectly by these systems. Any dysfunction of one system may have far-reaching and significant effects upon the nervous system because of this inherent relationship.

Structure determines function. Our bones are more than supports, our muscles more than pulleys, our nerves more than wiring, and our vessels more than fluid conduits. According to chiropractic principles, health care must embrace the relationship between structure and function in both its macroscopic and microscopic aspects.

The healthy human body has inherent healing powers and cannot be separated from consideration of the body as a total unit. This principle is ancient in origin and dates to the teachings of Hippocrates, the ancient Greek physician. Just as life may be defined as the ability to respond to a stimulus, health must be considered the ability to adapt to internal and external stresses. (Coulter, 1999)

Every person is an individual from fingerprints to body structure, function, response, adaptability, habits, and compulsions. All logical theory and therapy should be directed to recognition of individual differences and to the support of an individual's nature. Recognizing this, chiropractic approaches patients as unique individuals.

The Nature of Disease

All living cells possess the capacity to respond to external or internal environmental changes by performing special functions to secure proper adaptation and survival. In our body, the nervous system serves as a control system that coordinates cellular activities for adaptation to both normal and stressful external and internal changes and influences. Thus the nervous system serves a primary role in directing cell function in the never-ending process of adjusting to external and internal conditions.

William Boyd, M.D., in his classic work, *A Textbook of Pathology*, reminds us that "Disease, whether of the heart, kidney, or brain, is disturbed function, not merely disordered structure. For pathology in the modern sense is physiology gone wrong and not just the morphological changes called lesions." In "Disease, A Way of Life," published in *Perspectives in Biology and Medicine*, Stewart Wolf, M.D., states that "Disease is a reaction to, rather than an effect of, noxious forces."

Thus disease is the result of normal function that is not synchronized with environmental need. It is not necessarily the result of any new function. Sickness is not the result of what something does to the body, but what the body does about it because existing mechanical, chemical, and/or mental irritation of the neural and other coordinating systems prevents appropriate adaptation. Disease is not an entity in itself, but a process involving abnormal function and resulting in abnormal tissue changes.

Commonly encountered mechanical irritants include physical injuries, gravitational and occupational stress, postural defects and faults, developmental imbalances, unbalanced work or play, and deforming changes in the joints. Other irritants commonly encountered in our environment include the toxins of pathogenic microorganisms; drugs, pesticides, and other chemicals; radiation; noise; metabolic wastes; and other pollutants. In addition, the emotional and mental disturbances arising out of the effect of hostile human relations and of the personality's attempts to cope with stress are the principal psychic irritants in our society today.

When a person understands the basic nature of disease, that person will understand why chiropractors emphasize the health status of the nervous system. Since one of the basic causes of disease is adverse environmental irritation of the nervous system, it is apparent that any measure that will help to relieve such irritation, regardless of its nature, may constitute useful treatment. At times, the source of nerve irritation is very obvious, simple, and accessible, making the approach easy. Other times, the irritating factors may be complex, obscure, manifold, and inaccessible, posing a more complicated diagnostic problem.

Obviously no single method of assessment and treatment offers a panacea. However, one may be better suited to the problem than another, or a combined effort might be advisable. This places an enormous responsibility upon any physician, since he or she has to decide which therapy or therapies are indicated for the individual patient.

Human Ecology

Scientists have found that human beings live on a day-to-day basis with a host of viruses, bacteria, fungi, and parasites that are potentially disease-producing, but usually remain latent or harmless. A healthy body's defense system keeps the body in a state of health. A state of biologic equilibrium between health and illness can be upset by any change in the internal or external environment, such as sudden changes in weather, mental stress, overwork, nutritional deficiency, and other factors.

Freedom from infectious disease is not dependent upon the absence of microorganisms, since an environment that would kill all bacteria, viruses, and fungi would kill the patient, too. But freedom from disease is dependent upon maintaining normal function despite their presence. The body protects itself against harmful microorganisms by producing antibodies and other cell-defense mechanisms to destroy invading microbes and/or their products.

These phagocytes and antibodies are not independent entities. The nervous, endocrine, and circulatory systems influence their role. Hence, chiropractors contend that a significant approach to patient care is to ensure undisturbed function of the nervous system. Any environmental irritation of the nervous, endocrine, and immune systems can upset normal function and permit microorganisms that are already present in the body to initiate an infectious process. As well, malfunctions of muscular coordination have been known to precipitate more serious disorders.

The body's resistance to the invader is not accomplished by one body system, but by all body systems. Such resistance is the accumulated and coordinated forces of the body's totality—some known, some yet unknown.

Health science would be much simpler if a single disease could be attributed to a single cause. Unfortunately, this is not the case. We all live in a complex environment of potential microbial invasion, but only a minority of people become infected. Even many of the most virulent strains of pathogenic organisms do not infect every person exposed. Bodily resistance, acquired or inherited, and many other factors combine to determine whether an invading organism will result in noticeable infection.

Antibiotics and other potent medicines have certain beneficial effects in reducing bacterial populations. However, it has been shown that chemotherapy may also increase latent infection. As a chemical irritant to the nervous system capable of upsetting the equilibrium in minor infections, the antibiotic could trigger an unfavorable reaction and thus may produce complications. Some old diseases are disappearing, but new ones are appearing, possibly as the result of imprudent use of potent therapeutic agents.

Although the chiropractic profession has voiced its concern over the indiscriminate use of the "miracle" medications for several decades, it has only been in recent years that the scientific community and government agencies have also become openly concerned. The position of the chiropractic profession is not negative, but realistic and positive, compatible with the most advanced facts bearing upon the problems of human disease and disorder. Since its early beginning, chiropractic encouraged the use of optimum nutrition, fresh air, sunlight, exercise, and personal hygiene—all lifestyle factors that science is now recognizing as essential for the promotion of health and disease prevention.

The chiropractor is also a champion of slum clearance and adequate housing and advocates working conditions that avoid unnecessary structural, chemical, and fatigue stress. The chiropractor considers fear campaigns and other well-publicized situations leading to psychological stress a disservice to general health. As a proponent of rational public health measures, the D.C. encourages every effort that will decrease poverty or raise the level of living standards, general health, and physical fitness.

In broad terms, disease is the result of abnormal function, and abnormal function is the result of the body's inability to cope with stress. Such stress may be the result of any one or a combination of irritations: mechanical, thermal, chemical, hormonal, bacteriological, viral, parasitic, psychological, and so on. Susceptibility is determined by many factors; however, common external factors are environmental changes and virulent organisms, and common internal factors are the body's resistance and hereditary factors.

Chiropractors' Conservative Approach

Chiropractors approach the patient using conservative methods and do not use prescription drugs and surgery such as used in allopathic and osteopathic practice. The chiropractic approach endeavors to establish and maintain optimal body function by manually correcting abnormal structural relationships. Chiropractors assist the patient to use her/his own biologic reserves for a return to normal function. (Coulter, 1999) The D.C.'s special concern is the optimal coordination among the various systems of the body.

In addition to the manual therapies that chiropractors specialize in, most chiropractors advise and prescribe treatment relative to lifestyle, habits, and adverse environmental influences. Thus the chiropractor is concerned with the integrity of the entire body. The spinal column and adjacent tissues remain the D.C.'s primary interest. However, the D.C.'s armamentarium may include many more measures in addition to a corrective structural adjustment of the spinal column and pelvis.

The healing power of nature is a natural phenomenon recognized since the earliest civilizations. The power of the body to resist disease, heal its wounds, and maintain health has always been a fundamental concept in all the healing arts, regardless of theories and methods. Unfortunately, this basic concept has often not received widespread practical application. The chiropractic profession has been one of the most consistent advocates of the body's ability to maintain itself in a healthy state and to defend against many kinds of illness. Chiropractors use conservative, natural care to promote the body's natural defense mechanisms.

No single healing art offers a comprehensive solution to all the problems confronted in the health-care field. Chiropractic is no exception. If a patient needs surgery or medication, D.C.s will regularly refer patients for such care. However, the emphasis that the chiropractic profession places upon the importance of the nervous system, biomechanics, and body resistance are contributions that have yet to realize their full potential.

To summarize, the doctor of chiropractic places emphasis upon the importance of the body's biomechanics, especially that of the spine, and how its interplay with the nervous system affects many important body functions. The specific adjustment of the spine improves biomechanics and relieves associated nerve disorders. The focus is to optimize the patient's health through chiropractic care.

2

HISTORY OF CHIROPRACTIC

ONE OF THE features that makes chiropractic such an exciting profession is its venerable tradition of healing people through the use of natural care, primarily the adjustment of spinal and extremity joints. The birth of chiropractic, including its unique philosophy, was stimulated by various social factors present at the time of chiropractic's founding in the late 1800s.

Early Health Care in America

The practice of health care as we know it today is a relatively recent achievement. Many scientific discoveries that are now taken for granted occurred in the 1800s. Before this time, anyone who provided health care was called a "doctor," and the act of providing this care was termed the "practice of medicine." Some people did not use actual medicines to care for patients, but the terminology of the period did not change for many decades to come.

During America's colonial days, many doctors were without formal medical education and practiced their healing art along with other occupations such as barbers, ministers, and innkeepers. Self-educated lay doctors were typical in American culture for a long time because few graduates of European universities, who were of the upper social classes, were willing to endure the hardships of the New World.

In America, formal medical education was slow in starting, and early medical schools had short curricula (for example, six months) and were proprietary institutions. Apprenticeship or self-training was the usual and almost exclusive path to becoming a medical doctor in most areas of the country. Meager training in the healing arts existed until long after the Civil War. In fact, it was not until the middle 1800s that states began to introduce laws licensing the practitioners of medicine.

Allopathic care from the colonial days and into the second half of the 1800s was quite limited because all of the scientific advancements that we are familiar with today had yet to be discovered. Doctors typically provided first aid for broken bones, cuts, dislocated joints, and various other kinds of trauma. For infectious diseases, disorders of the internal organs, and other maladies, little could be done. What was offered was known as "heroic medicine." (Wardwell, 1992) Heroic medicine involved primitive means by which the doctor attempted to purge the body of "impurities."

Some of the standard heroic methods of the time included draining blood from patients' veins (bloodletting), administering chemicals that would induce vomiting and diarrhea (cathartics and emetics), and crude surgeries that did not use antiseptic techniques. Medicinal preparations were mostly proprietary, containing secret ingredients, but often laced with strong doses of alcohol or opiates and poisons such as mercury or arsenic. Advocates of heroic medicine recommended that the strongest doses of these drugs be given to the sickest patient; thus treatment was often much more harmful or deadly than the disease for which it was prescribed.

Patients were well advised to seek gentler alternatives, and these alternative health-care methods began to flourish in the 1800s. Alternative practitioners were popular; they offered more conservative and less potentially damaging healing treatments. These health-care providers used a variety of natural healing agents to help patients, including dietary modifications, the use of herbs and plants as medicines, exercise, bonesetting and manipulation, religious healing, magnetic healing, sunshine, and mineral baths. The most popular alternatives that arose during this time included homeopathy, osteopathy, naturopathy, and chiropractic. (Wardwell, 1992)

During the middle and late 1800s, practitioners of medicine began to organize and form societies, such as the founding of the American Medical Association (AMA) in 1847. One of the goals of the AMA was to improve medical education and to begin to standardize medical practice. In doing so, health-care practitioners who used alternative practices were seen by organized medicine to be unorthodox and were considered outsiders. For this reason, many alternative providers were jailed for practicing "medicine" without a license, since there were no laws to govern the practice of alternative health approaches. Summarily, organized medicine, called "orthodox medicine" at that time, developed a sense of cultural dominance, especially when new scientific discoveries began to influence medical practice. (Wardwell, 1992)

Since that time, the three contemporary clinical professions— chiropractic, osteopathy, and allopathic medicine—have developed in relative isolation from one another. Each group evolved primarily in a clinical setting with a self-generated terminology specific to the history of the particular clinical school of thought.

The Birth of Chiropractic

Many significant achievements in medical science occurred in the late 1800s. The tubercle bacillus (the bacterial agent of tuberculosis) was not identified until the late 1880s, and Pasteur had established only his germ theory in the 1860s. Yet Lister's introduction of antiseptic surgery (for example, washing hands prior to performing surgery and using antiseptics) was still meeting conservative medical opposition. It was not until the mid-1890s that x-rays were discovered and that Harvey Cushing brought the first blood pressure instrument to the United States. Medical science was still crude; yet there was an air of innovation, and many important discoveries and inventions were on the horizon.

It was into this environment that chiropractic was born. Chiropractic was founded by Daniel David Palmer of Davenport, Iowa. He had been born of English and German ancestry, in the small Canadian town of Pickering, Ontario, just east of Toronto. In 1865, at the age of twenty, he moved to the United States. After engaging in several occupations, including those of grocer, beekeeper, horticulturist, and grade school teacher, he became interested in healing the sick. (Wardwell, 1992)

Palmer was inspired in his healing approach by many of the alternative practices of the period. One of the most popular practices was called magnetic healing. Derived from the work of Anton Mesmer, M.D., of Europe, magnetic healing involved the "laying on of hands" to transfer "vital magnetic energy" from the doctor to the patient. Palmer was most influenced by the work of Paul Caster, an internationally known practitioner of magnetic healing, and his extensive readings on the subject. D. D. Palmer opened an office as a magnetic healer around 1885. (Keating et al., 1998)

D. D. Palmer practiced his art with unusual success for about a decade prior to his transformation of magnetic healing into the practice of chiropractic. Dr. Palmer helped hundreds of patients as a magnetic healer and opened an infirmary where people could stay for extended periods while they received his treatment. Dr. Palmer provided his patients with clean accommodations and good, healthy food to eat. Palmer was an intelligent, yet somewhat extraordinary nonconformist, with an intuitive perception of the world about him. Although he had started with no more than an eighth grade education like the traditional medical doctors at that time, he was a voracious reader, stocked his personal library with the best medical texts of the time, and consulted these liberally.

D. D. Palmer began to practice just a few years after the state of Iowa licensed medical doctors. As a rough-hewn frontier doctor and intense individualist, his interest in ways to heal the sick led him to be critical of the confusion existing in the healing arts of his day. He believed that many common drugs and heroic therapies were actually toxic stressors to patients who were already weakened by illness. He thought resistance to disease had more to do with the person's vital energy and overall health. In agreement with Hippocratic philosophy, he did not believe that the cause of illness was strictly an agent external to the body, but considered "dis-ease" a natural response to an abnormal situation. These thoughts were to have a profound effect upon his later life, his teachings, and the formation of the chiropractic profession.

As a self-taught student of anatomy and physiology, Palmer constantly improved his practice. He began to notice that if he made quick thrusts to his patients' spines, they seemed to heal sooner than when he used his other magnetic methods. In early 1895 he made a clinical observation. Harvey Lillard, a building superintendent where Palmer practiced, entered Palmer's office. Mr. Lillard had a hearing deficit originating several years earlier when he strained himself working in a cramped position. Lillard mentioned to Palmer that at the time of the strain he felt something "give" in his spine immediately before he lost his hearing.

Palmer examined Lillard's spine and found a painful, prominent vertebra in the midthoracic spine. Using the spinous process of the vertebra as a lever, Palmer applied a sharp thrust to it in an attempt to help Mr. Lillard. This new idea of delivering a quick, isolated thrust to the spine of a patient later came to be known as the chiropractic adjustment. Lillard reported that his hearing improved greatly. Palmer immediately began to try to understand the relationship of health and disease to his new form of hands-on healing. (Wardwell, 1992)

With careful study of more patients, Palmer noted that many other types of disorders improved with such "hand" (i.e., manual) treatments. Palmer decided to rename his approach to helping patients. In search for a name, Palmer asked one of his patients, the Reverend Samuel Weed, if he knew of Greek words meaning "done by hand." Weed offered *cheiro* (hand) *practikos* (practice), and from these roots the term *chiropractic* was derived. While this term has remained unchanged throughout the years, Palmer was to revise his theories of chiropractic several times up to his death, incorporating revisions as the new chiropractic technology and science evolved. However, Dr. Palmer's theories of chiropractic always centralized on the relationship between the nervous system and health and how this relationship could be influenced by chiropractic adjustments.

In the coming decades, chiropractic became more sophisticated: a formal education program evolved, schools developed entrance requirements, and supporters fought for state laws governing practice. However, not unlike many before him who advocated a new, holistic philosophy, Dr. Palmer's teachings were controversial among the orthodox medical community.

Did Chiropractors Invent Spinal Manipulation?

Although the exact origin of therapeutic manipulation is lost in antiquity, anthropological findings and interpretation of ancient documents indicate that manipulation has existed throughout the world since the beginning of recorded time.

Some of the earliest indications of manipulation are demonstrated within the ancient Chinese Kong Fou document written about 2700 B.C. Greek papyruses dating back to 1500 B.C. gave instructions on the maneuvering of the lower extremities in the treatment of low-back conditions. There appears to be no single origin of the art. Manipulation was practiced by the ancient Japanese, the Indians of Asia, as well as the early Egyptians, Babylonians, Syrians, Hindus, Tibetans, and Tahitians for centuries. (Peterson and Wiese, 1995)

Ancient American Indian hieroglyphics demonstrate "back walking," in which the ailing person would lie down and have his or her spine manipulated by the feet of others. The early natives of Polynesian Islands had children walk on the backs of the sick. Explorers reported observations of therapeutic manipulations by Islanders in the 1500s. Thus the use of manipulation has been established as part of health care throughout the world. (Peterson and Wiese, 1995)

It is believed that during the Middle Ages a form of manipulation called "bonesetting" was handed down from father to son or mother to daughter and was practiced by at least one person in most communities of Europe, North Africa, and Asia. Often highly skilled but without the benefit of formal education, the bonesetters of Europe flourished. Their success, however, did not meet the general approval of the orthodox medical community. As time went on, the bonesetters of Europe and Asia acquired great fame as healers. In the January 5, 1865, issue of *British Medical Journal*, the noted surgeon Sir James Paget wrote an article entitled "Cases That Bonesetters Cure." Wharton Hood, M.D., followed with more on the manipulative arts in the *Lancet*, but even this recognition did little to stimulate objective investigation by the medical aristocracy of the era.

Bonesetting was also practiced in the United States. Bonesetters have been reported in some Native American Indian tribes and are also known to have practiced in Mexico. D. D. Palmer even states that he learned bonesetting while he was a magnetic healer. In fact, several chiropractic families today come from a long line of bonesetters. (Wardwell, 1992)

In 1874 Andrew Taylor Still, also a bonesetter, was manipulating patients in his newly declared practice of osteopathy. Soon he opened a school to teach others the practice of osteopathy, which held the theory that the body was a machine and could be healed like one. He stated that the body would release its own internal pharmaceuticals to aid healing after manipulation was performed. Thus osteopathy predates chiropractic by a few years. Yet osteopaths also began using medicines and surgical techniques in their practices. So, over time, especially by the middle 1900s, it became difficult to differentiate a medical doctor from an osteopath, unless the osteopath placed a strong emphasis on manipulation in his or her practice. (Wardwell, 1992)

In the early days, chiropractic and osteopathic adjustments were similar. However, the philosophies of the two professions were different. Chiropractic focused on the patient's health being maintained by the nervous system, and osteopathy focused on the body's release of an internal pharmacopoeia. Through their dedication to the art, by the early 1900s, chiropractors had evolved adjusting into a highly specialized and specific art form.

Contributions of Early Civilizations to Health Care

Both Eastern and Western cultures had much to do with building the foundation of the healing arts, and knowing about some of these early approaches helps us better understand the position of chiropractic in modern-day health care.

The Chinese as far back as 2838 B.C. offered important advances with their development of manipulation, massage, the measurement of movement, acupuncture and acupressure, pulse diagnosis, herbs, and many medicines. Records are clear that manipulation, massage, and acupuncture were practiced by the Japanese at least as early as 600 B.C.

Different viewpoints among the healing arts today can be traced to their origins in history. Within some primitive societies, it was believed that the one cause of disease could be found in some outside morbid influence that entered the victim. Thus rose the belief in hexes, demons, and other evil forces. On the other hand, some societies looked upon illness as an abstraction of the soul from the victim's body. Thus from these two basic premises evolved the various theories that supported or contradicted the philosophies that are argued even today among health scientists. These two philosophies represent thought as to whether disease is an invasion from outside the body, or if disease is a manifestation of a body that can not cope or adapt to meet the demands of its environment.

Hippocrates served as chief physician and teacher at the Coan School, located on the island of Cos near Asia Minor. The Hippocratic approach was argued by a nearby rival school at Cnidus, where the disease rather than the patient was emphasized. At Cnidus, the patient's condition was viewed as an accident to the patient, coming from outside the body. Contrarily, Hippocrates centered on the patient, and disease was not looked upon as an invading entity such as a demon, but as a changeable condition of the patient's body—thus a battle between illness and the natural self-healing tendency of the body.

Although Hippocrates knew how to use many potent medicines, his scheme of treatment was usually confined to assisting the body's natural responses with mild remedies. Hippocrates founded his teachings on his firm belief that while the causes of disease could come from either outside or inside the victim, "it is our natures that are the physicians of our diseases." He stressed that a human being must be treated as a whole, that the ultimate curative forces are within, that we should study the entire patient and her or his environment, and that we should approach sickness with the eye of the naturalist.

Hippocrates was a prolific writer; at least seventy books on healing are attributed to him, including *Manipulation and Importance to Good Health* and *On Setting Joints by Leverage*. He also recognized the importance of spinal manipulation. Emphasizing the importance of the spine, he wrote, "Get knowledge of the spine, for this is the requisite for many diseases." *Summum bonum*—the highest good—is to remove the cause, taught Hippocrates. Nature must heal; the physician can only remove the obstruction. Much of chiropractic's patient-centered and natural approach is reflected in Hippocratic roots.

Chiropractic Pioneers

D. D. Palmer publicly communicated his concepts about a major cause of disease, his theories about health and its maintenance, and the results of his practice. He published numerous newspapers from his office emphasizing these points. The orthodox allopathic community did not like or accept Dr. Palmer's advertising. He had a tendency to talk about how he succeeded with cases not cured by medical doctors, and advertising a practice in this manner was against the ethical code of organized medicine at that time. By now relationships between orthodox doctors and alternative practitioners were strained; this did nothing to help Palmer's cause. The members of the medical establishment fought Dr. Palmer's approach, and he fought back with conviction.

However, the growth of chiropractic did not depend upon making its basic concepts acceptable to medical practitioners of the times. Palmer took his case to the public, and the profession grew because of the enthusiastic response of the patients.

While it is known that D. D. Palmer had taught his methods of magnetic healing to others before the birth of chiropractic, he opened his first official school in 1896 in Davenport, Iowa. He called it Palmer's School of Magnetic Cure and proceeded to teach chiropractic there, even though the school's name did not have the word *chiropractic* in it. The name of the school was soon changed to the Palmer School and Cure in 1897. (Keating et al., 1998)

Five of Dr. Palmer's first fifteen graduates to receive a diploma recognizing them as doctors of chiropractic were medical or osteopathic physicians: Drs. Seeley, Brown, Davis, Hender, and Walton.

William M. P. Brown, M.D., D.C., became the first clinic director under Dr. Palmer. Andrew P. Davis, M.D., D.O., D.C., became the author of one of the first texts on osteopathy. Later, A. B. Hender, M.D., D.C., became one of the first deans of the school and served in this capacity for decades. (Keating et al., 1998)

It was not long before new chiropractic institutions were started by some of D. D. Palmer's early graduates. Dr. Palmer had, in fact, encouraged this by noting on their diplomas that they were competent to "Teach and Practice" chiropractic. However, Dr. Palmer may not have been prepared for his graduates to begin teaching new chiropractic theories and methods, and this was not favorable to him. He believed strongly that chiropractic was to be done by hand, as defined by the word *chiropractic* itself. When graduates began incorporating other forms of care, including the use of machines and naturopathy, into chiropractic, Palmer was quite upset. Nonetheless, such challenges to the blossoming profession may have helped it grow by suggesting other mechanisms for how chiropractic worked and advancing new means to help patients.

Solon Langworthy, D.C., one of Palmer's early graduates, succeeded in several advancements of the chiropractic profession during the early days. In 1903 he opened his American School of Chiropractic and Nature Cure in Cedar Rapids, Iowa. This was the first serious rival school to Palmer's. He also started the first chiropractic journal, called *Backbone*, that same year. Langworthy is credited as being the first to use the term *subluxation* in the chiropractic literature, and he was instrumental in pioneering investigations into the anatomy of the spine. Langworthy was joined at his school by two other early Palmer graduates, Oakley Smith, D.C., and Minora Paxson, D.C. Langworthy's school was one of the earlier institutions to begin using therapeutic agents in addition to spinal adjustment to help patients.

The trio of Langworthy, Smith, and Paxson was extremely productive. Together they published the very first textbook about chiropractic, entitled *Modernized Chiropractic*, in 1906. At their school they also offered the first structured chiropractic curriculum, consisting of four five-month terms. (Keating et al., 1998) This in itself was a huge accomplishment, because until that time chiropractors had been trained in the same apprentice type of education that was prominent in medical education in the 1800s. Although their school does not exist today, the influence of these doctors was great on the new profession.

Among D. D. Palmer's early students was his son Bartlett Joshua Palmer. "BJ," as he liked to be called, earned his D.C. in 1902. BJ eventually took over the Palmer School from his father only to find that it was in financial trouble. He soon turned the school around and developed it into the largest chiropractic school in the world at that time.

BJ was a very unique individual and was known for integrating popular culture into his management style. He constantly introduced change to the Palmer School. (Maynard, 1991) In 1908 he revealed a new chiropractic adjusting technique to the profession that he claimed was more specific than the procedures taught previously. By 1910 he had introduced diagnostic x-rays into the school clinic. Among other things, he started a radio station at the Palmer School and used it to spread the message of chiropractic over the airwaves. (Keating, 1997)

BJ was also responsible for starting a nationwide defense system for chiropractors who were sent to jail for practicing chiropractic. This was a terrible period of persecution for the profession. Organized medicine attempted to eliminate chiropractic by jailing chiropractors for practicing medicine, even though they were actually practicing chiropractic, not medicine. BJ also started one of the profession's national organizations, known today as the International Chiropractors Association, and he accomplished many other things. (Keating, 1997) Certainly BJ's life cannot be condensed into just a few paragraphs. Entire books have been written about this charismatic chiropractic leader, and the reader is encouraged to explore them. (Keating, 1997 and Maynard, 1991)

A number of other early graduates were instrumental in securing the chiropractic profession. John F. A. Howard, D.C., graduated from Palmer in 1906 and opened the National School of Chiropractic that same year in the very same building where D. D. Palmer had adjusted Harvey Lillard. (Keating et al., 1998) Within a few years, Howard moved the school to the Chicago area, where it remains today as the National University of Health Sciences. Howard immediately began incorporating physiotherapeutic agents in his practice and teaching of chiropractic. For this reason, many regard National as the birthplace of this approach to chiropractic care.

Thomas H. Storey, D.C., graduated from Palmer in 1901. Upon his return to Los Angeles, he was instrumental in training Charles Cale, D.C., who opened the Los Angeles College of Chiropractic, now the Southern California University of Health Sciences. (Keating et al., 1998) Many others like him crossed the country to found chiropractic colleges of their own. Students of chiropractic receive further education in the history of the profession at most chiropractic colleges. Check the curricula of the colleges you are considering if this is an area of interest for you.

D. D. Palmer died in Los Angeles in 1913, but not before he had instilled his concepts and enthusiasm for this new science, directly or indirectly, in the minds and hearts of those who would develop the profession into one of the largest healing arts in the world. For the next few decades, this awakening profession would produce an abundance of practitioners and schools that varied in their expansion, contraction, and interpretation of D. D. Palmer's teachings and writings. Thus chiropractic was refined as it passed through succeeding classes of students, teachers, and professional leaders.

Licensing

The first state law licensing chiropractors was passed in Kansas in 1913, and by 1931 thirty-nine states had given doctors of chiropractic legal recognition. However, achieving nationwide licensure was not an easy process, and many chiropractors were abused, fined, and jailed until their rights to practice chiropractic were legalized. Today chiropractors are licensed in all fifty American states and in more than eighty countries worldwide. This section describes how these laws were formed. (See Chapter 6 for more information regarding current licensing laws.)

Because chiropractors had to legally fight for licensure, licenses to practice chiropractic were obtained differently in all fifty states in America. For this reason, each state has slightly different requirements for licensure, although today a more standardized process is being used.

Once licensing laws were established, many graduates were required to take examinations in the basic sciences. These were known as Basic Science Laws. The intention of these examinations was to determine if chiropractors had sufficient basic science knowledge, which some governing boards believed was a good indicator of a doctor's ability to practice. Chiropractors, medical doctors, and osteopaths were required to take and pass these exams to receive a license in their state. (Keating et al., 1998)

Eventually, when it became widely recognized that chiropractors performed as well as, and in many situations better than, other health-care providers, the responsibility to administer these examinations was relinquished to the chiropractic profession.

Finally the National Board of Chiropractic Examiners (NBCE) was created. The National Board of Chiropractic Examiners is the principal testing agency for the chiropractic profession. It was established in 1963 after studies showed that scores from standardized national examinations, when developed and administered according to established testing industry guidelines, can provide certain benefits to a health-care profession. Among these are:

- The safeguarding of uniformly high standards of competency among practitioners
- An easing of the burden on state licensing agencies
- Facilitation of the licensure process for incoming practitioners
- Enhanced professional credibility

In providing standardized academic and clinical testing services to the chiropractic profession, the NBCE develops, administers, analyzes, scores, and reports results from various examinations. The National Board test results are among the criteria utilized by state licensing agencies in determining whether applicants satisfy that state's minimum qualifications for licensure.

In its role as a national and international testing agency, the NBCE represents no particular chiropractic approach or philosophy. The agency's examinations are formulated according to information provided collectively by all of the chiropractic colleges, the state licensing agencies, field practitioners, and subject specialists.

The evolution of chiropractic licensure continues. Instead of just the basic science boards, chiropractors must now pass the NBCE examinations. In later years, a second part was added to ensure competency in clinical practice topics such as diagnosis, patient management, and radiology. A separate physiotherapeutics part was also added to ensure that graduates demonstrate a sufficient level of knowledge in the use of these modalities. Finally, in the last decade, a hands-on practical examination was added to test doctors in their interactions with patients and proficiency in clinical care. This is known as part four of the NBCE.

In addition to passing the required parts of the NBCE examinations for the state(s) that he or she wishes to practice in, a D.C. may need to meet other requirements. (These issues are also covered in Chapter 6.)

Development of Educational Standards

The importance of quality education was recognized by early chiropractic educators; however, organized efforts to improve chiropractic education were not undertaken until the early 1930s, when a Committee on Education was introduced by Dr. Claude O. Watkins of the National Chiropractic Association (NCA), now the American Chiropractic Association (ACA). (Keating et al., 1998)

The Council of State Chiropractic Examining Boards also began to improve chiropractic education at about the same time as the NCA, and in 1938 these two groups established a Committee on Educational Standards. As many as thirty-seven institutions of various sizes were in existence at the time. In 1939 the Committee on Educational Standards completed work on educational criteria that were presented to serve as guides for the approval of the chiropractic colleges. In 1941 the Committee on Educational Standards issued its first list of institutions with status, which consisted of twelve provisionally approved colleges. In 1947 the NCA Council on Education, forerunner of today's Council on Chiropractic Education, was formed by institutional representatives and members of the Committee on Educational Standards.

During the twenty-year period from 1941 to 1961, the Council on Education strengthened chiropractic education significantly. Many weaker institutions were merged with other schools to create stronger academic programs. A number of the grossly substandard schools were simply closed. By 1961 the number of chiropractic colleges was reduced to ten. In 1971 the Council was incorporated as an autonomous national organization, the Council on Chiropractic Education (CCE), and it continues to function as such today. (Wardwell, 1992)

Recognition by the U.S. Office of Education (USOE) was important. Initial contact with the USOE by the CCE's parent organization was made in 1952, and an official application for recognition was filed in 1959. The USOE's suggestions for strengthening academic standards and procedures were implemented, and in 1969 an unofficial filing of materials was made with the USOE, which resulted in further suggestions for change. In August 1972 the CCE filed its formal application with the USOE, and in August 1974 the CCE was first listed as a "nationally recognized accrediting agency" by the U.S. Commissioner of Education. (Wardwell, 1992) Periodically, the Commissioner renews recognition of the CCE.

From its simplest beginnings to its exciting present state, chiropractic has been and continues to be a dynamic profession. The profession has demonstrated incredible resolve in ensuring that this powerful, health-enhancing form of health care is available to people in need. Oftentimes we forget the struggles of chiropractic pioneers to create such a notable profession. Whether your future involves establishing new licensing laws in foreign lands or merely improving the availability and access to chiropractic care in your home state, there are plenty of opportunities for you to further enhance the chiropractic profession.

3

CHIROPRACTIC AS A
PROFESSIONAL CAREER

INCREASINGLY WIDE ACCEPTANCE and a rapidly growing population make the future of chiropractic a nearly boundless one. Chiropractic is a rapidly growing profession offering a career of rare opportunity and service to the dedicated doctor. In return, the profession provides security, prestige, and excellent income to practitioners.

Professional and Economic Rewards

A career in chiropractic offers real, lasting satisfaction in patient care and a rewarding income. The D.C. enjoys the advantages of a profession that is well established, one that ranks high in prestige and service and does not limit opportunity, income, or challenge. Chiropractic also offers opportunities of community service and leadership.

Independence

According to the National Board of Chiropractic Examiners' *2000 Job Analysis of Chiropractic*, 63 percent of doctors of chiropractic practice in their own, independent office. (Christensen et al., 2000) Such D.C.s are their own employers, and, therefore, their own managers. They establish their own hours and work habits and are able to arrange their hours by appointment to suit their patients and personal and family needs. They determine when they will take their vacations and their days off. With this independence, the D.C. has the responsibility to generate his or her own income and, therefore, must build the practice to a volume that meets personal goals. In 2002, chiropractors were rated thirteenth as the best job for self-employed workers. (jist.com)

Group Practice

It is becoming more common for D.C.s to be employed by a company or organization, such as a health maintenance organization, government agency, or hospital setting. In these situations, the chiropractor may not have as much independence as he or she would have in an independent practice; however, these D.C.s usually receive a salary and do not have to put forth as much energy in building a practice as would an independent practitioner.

Many hospital staffs now grant chiropractors limited coadmitting privileges. Many health-care authorities predict that the outcomes of chiropractic involvement by the various hospitals currently granting staff privileges will determine the future for increased hospital participation.

There is no question that as chiropractic demonstrates its effective, conservative management in various ailments under hospital supervision, there will be an increased demand for chiropractic by both society and the medical community.

Location

Chiropractors have offices in large cities, small towns, and rural areas. Chiropractic offices are usually found in downtown office buildings, freestanding offices, and health professional complexes. Many D.C.s choose to set up interdisciplinary practices in offices with other health providers such as medical doctors, dieticians, massage therapists, and physical therapists. Because chiropractic practice is a "low-tech, high-touch" profession, chiropractors can easily set up practices in locations that bring them closer to their clientele. Chiropractors can also be found in fitness centers, health centers within large corporations, and even in mobile offices.

Prestige

Doctors of chiropractic enjoy the respect of their patients and community. They earn the gratitude of all for fulfilling an honorable and needed function; that of maintaining the health and welfare of the people. They are looked up to as leaders and, as such, have the opportunity to make many friends and to achieve social and civic prominence. Chiropractic office hours allow ample time to enjoy a full schedule of social, business, and professional activities. The personal contacts made professionally and socially often enable D.C.s to reach positions of leadership.

Income

The chiropractic profession is not interested in attracting students who are solely invested in financial gain. Rather, chiropractic wants earnest men and women who will find gratification in contributing to human betterment. However, financial stability should certainly be taken into account when determining a career. The earning potential of a doctor of chiropractic is as good as and often better than that of other professions. In 2002, chiropractic was listed as the sixteenth highest paying job (jist.com).

According to the U.S. Department of Labor, Bureau of Labor Statistics (bls.gov), the average annual wage for D.C.s in 2001 was $76,870, and the seventy-fifth percentile was $112,580. The American Chiropractic Association reports that the average annual income in the year 2000 was about $81,500. The Sixth Annual Salary and Expense Survey, published by *Chiropractic Economics*, polled 535 chiropractors and found similar results, reporting in 2003 that the average D.C. had a net personal income between $75,000 and $89,000 (chiroeco.com/article/2003/issue6/survey .html).

As in other professions, financial success depends upon many factors: the individual characteristics of the practitioner, the doctor's ability to apply her or his knowledge, the doctor's personality, the location of practice, and local economic conditions. However, statistics show that professional people overall, regardless of personal circumstances, enjoy a greater degree of security and higher income than any other group.

What Are the Career Opportunities?

A career in chiropractic offers many different opportunities for professionals to focus their efforts. In previous decades, the only option for chiropractic graduates was to enter general private practice. Although this is still the most popular option, opportunities exist for specialization, further education, and careers in research and education.

Job Prospects

According to the U.S. Department of Labor, Bureau of Labor Statistics (bls.gov), job prospects are good for students who enter the practice of chiropractic. The Bureau reports that "Employment of chiropractors is expected to grow faster than average for all occupations through the year 2010 as consumer demand for alternative healthcare grows." The use of alternative health-care services has grown at an astounding rate in the past decade, and chiropractic is the most frequently used of these services. For example, between the years 1990 and 1997, the use of alternative care grew from an estimated 33.8 percent of Americans to 42.1 percent, and the upward trend has continued. This growth represents a 47.3 percent increase in total visits to alternative care providers in just seven years, and a great majority of these patients visited chiropractors. (Eisenberg et al., 1998) Wolsko and colleagues reported in a 2003 article published in the journal *Spine* that approximately one-third of all complementary care visits were for neck and back pain, and that chiropractors saw most of these patients. (Wolsko et al., 2003)

According to census figures and a survey made by the American Chiropractic Association, there is approximately one doctor of chiropractic serving every group of six thousand people in the United States. A more desirable ratio would be one doctor of chiropractic for every four thousand people. Thus there is an urgent demand for an immediate increase in the number of doctors of chiropractic in the United States, Canada, and several foreign countries. Literally hundreds of towns that could adequately support a doctor of chiropractic are without one.

Few cities of any size, even the largest, have enough doctors of chiropractic in ratio to the population. Currently D.C.s provide a significant amount of health-care service to rural areas that are undergoing shortages in health professions personnel. There are presently about sixty-five thousand licensed D.C.s in the United States, and this number is projected to grow to one hundred thousand by the year 2010. (Meeker and Haldeman, 2002) Not only is chiropractic among the least crowded of all professions, each year expanded service opportunities are opened to those in the profession. Such opportunities are outlined in this chapter.

General Practice

Chiropractic is a broad field. The clinical practice of chiropractic has demonstrated effectiveness for a number of diseases and disorders. Many chiropractors believe that general practice offers the greatest inducements and rewards. In general practice, a doctor of chiropractic is given the opportunity to use the full scope of his or her professional preparation.

In general practice, the D.C. serves patients of all ages, helps them learn how to live healthy lives, and cares for a variety of problems. The most common problems for which people seek chiropractic care are low-back and neck pain, and headaches. However, oftentimes patients have other or additional problems, such as problems with the arms, legs, or viscera that the chiropractor can manage. With the primary health problems in America being related to lifestyle factors such as diet and exercise, the D.C. is in an optimum position to help patients learn how to prevent these disorders. Of course, if it is necessary, the D.C. refers patients to other health-care providers when needed, and his or her education provides the training required to make such decisions.

Because of the increasing complexities in health care and the rapid technological advances in chemotherapy and surgical procedures, more and more allopathic and osteopathic practitioners are entering specialties, leaving a dire need for the general practitioner, especially in rural communities. Increasingly, D.C.s are fulfilling the role of family doctor. The reason for this is threefold: first, the chiropractor's approach to the patient as a total being; second, the fact that more than 50 percent of chiropractic doctors are located in rural and suburban areas; and third, because the doctor/patient relationship under chiropractic care is often more personal. Several studies have substantiated this latter point.

The majority of newly graduated and licensed chiropractors prepare for private practice by associating themselves with well-established general practitioners. This relationship often grows out of the field practice experience that chiropractic students are required to perform during their last year of chiropractic college. Salaries vary, depending on geographic location; initial associate-ships usually combine a salary with the opportunity to receive a percentage of income from the new patients that the new D.C. brings into the practice. Other new D.C.s may become staff members in group practices where there is a growing demand for qualified professional personnel. Due to the rising costs of office equipment, furnishings, and facilities, association with an established practice offers an opportunity to enter practice without a large financial investment.

Specialties

Although it is true that the majority of doctors of chiropractic choose general practice, there is ample opportunity within the profession for development in a special field of interest. A chiropractic physician may choose to specialize in orthopedics, radiology and diagnostic imaging, sports chiropractic, pediatrics, occupational injuries, personal and occupational injuries, nutritional consultation, or other special areas of interest. Many doctors of chiropractic have had outstanding success in their selected fields of specialty. This is particularly noteworthy since there has been a trend in recent years toward specialization in all the health professions, especially in practices located in highly populated urban areas.

Educational programs exist for D.C.s to learn about the vast array of specialty topics after they graduate from chiropractic college. Aspiring specialists must attend a required number of courses in the specialty and pass certifying examinations before being designated a specialist. Typically, such specialists are called diplomates in the chiropractic profession. Diplomate education is regulated by various specialty-certifying organizations. A D.C. specializing in sports chiropractic, for example, is designated a diplomate of the American Chiropractic Board of Sports Physicians. This process takes several years of postgraduate education, but the D.C. completes the program with in-depth knowledge of a particular area and may better serve his or her community with these skills. A few of these specialties are highlighted here as examples, and websites for many specialties can be found in Appendix A.

Chiropractic Radiologists

A number of chiropractors devote their entire practice to the taking and interpreting of diagnostic x-rays. These D.C.s also interpret other forms of imaging, such as magnetic resonance imaging and CAT scans. Chiropractic radiologists are renowned for their skills in evaluating imaging of the neuromusculoskeletal system and provide a valuable consulting service to chiropractic practitioners.

Nutritional Specialists

In addition to the correction of biomechanical faults, the development of good posture habits, and the necessity for regular exercise, nutrition plays an important role in maintaining health. Nourishing food that builds bone and muscle and maintains nerve and blood integrity is essential to good health. Education in proper nutrition is an important part of the curriculum at each accredited chiropractic college. However, some D.C.s select nutrition as a postgraduate specialty to complement their general practice.

Dietary management under chiropractic care is thus often necessary to see that the diet provides proper nutrition to help the body function at its maximum potential and heal quickly when under physical or emotional stress. Too often in our society, a well-balanced diet has been replaced by highly processed, fatty foods, such as fast foods, sugary snacks, and TV dinners. Chiropractic nutritionists learn how to analyze and modify their patients' diets to provide optimum nutrition.

Sports Chiropractors

One of the fastest-growing specialties in the chiropractic profession deals with the prevention and management of sport-related injuries. Because of chiropractic's emphasis upon structural/functional relationships in health and disease processes, and because of its natural, drugless approach to help people function at their optimum, there is a good relationship between chiropractic and sports.

The involvement of sports chiropractors has led to several contributions in protective gear and trauma management in contact sports, athletic health maintenance, therapy, and enhanced rehabilitation after injury.

Although chiropractic contributions in this area have been made for many years, the public press has brought great attention to the profession's unique approach. Chiropractors serve as recognized doctors at the Olympic Games, Pan-American Games, and at the collegiate and professional levels of competition. Many sports chiropractors serve as team doctors for local athletic groups and find this practice very rewarding. Because of their personal experiences with chiropractic care, several outstanding athletes have entered the chiropractic profession.

Personal and Occupational Injury Specialists

Many Americans carry health and accident insurance or other third-party payment plans that cover all or part of their costs for health-care services. There are many types of insurance. Most pay for chiropractic services; a few do not. Third-party payment for chiropractic care is becoming more popular each year and is expected to receive full coverage in the future. Those programs operated through state and federal agencies for special groups are also expected to increase. Some are designed to help veterans and service people and their dependents; some are designed for the aged and the indigent.

Chiropractic Pediatricians

Some chiropractors find caring for children very rewarding. Chiropractic colleges offer introductory courses in pediatrics in the regular curricula, but the expert management of children is a growing field in the chiropractic profession.

Chiropractic pediatricians help in the correction of faulty body mechanics during the stages of childhood development. Active children are particularly prone to spinal subluxation because they are energetic, impatient, and have an innocent disregard for caution.

Spinal disorders often are the result of twists, sudden turns, awkward lifts and postural positions, and jolts to the body during ordinary activity. Pediatricians also counsel their patients in proper childhood lifestyles, such as good nutrition, posture, and regular checkups.

Some D.C.s also help pregnant mothers cope with the many health disorders such as headaches, backaches, leg pains, and lower-extremity circulatory disturbances that often accompany pregnancy. During pregnancy there is a natural change within the pelvic structures, particularly in the last trimester, along with an accompanying change in weight distribution that can cause low-back pain, and because of the pregnancy the use of pain medication is ill-advised. In association with regular obstetrical care, periodic chiropractic spinal checks and adjustments throughout the course of pregnancy have shown excellent clinical results in either reducing or eliminating such disorders, as well as in easing the labor or delivery.

Residencies

Several chiropractic colleges offer residencies that can be pursued after one has a D.C. degree. Residencies offer opportunities for the chiropractor to learn advanced knowledge and skills and complete further education. Typical residencies last approximately three years. During this time, the resident usually works toward completing a postgraduate diplomate in a specialty field, or toward a graduate academic degree, such as a master's degree. The programs vary widely from college to college.

Programs often leading to specialty diplomate status include radiology and diagnostic imaging, clinical sciences, pediatrics, rehabilitation, and sports chiropractic. Programs leading to a graduate degree include research, exercise physiology and sports science, and other areas of interest. Usually a resident is able to defer his or her student loans during the residency period. If you are potentially interested in residency programs, inquire with the colleges that you are considering to see what opportunities may exist.

Education

For those whose interests and talents qualify them, there is excellent opportunity to teach in chiropractic colleges in the United States, Canada, and abroad. With the expansion of chiropractic across the globe, there are now more chiropractic institutions outside of the United States than inside, providing more opportunities than ever before in chiropractic education. Serving as an educator is a most rewarding way of expressing chiropractic skills. Many chiropractic educators maintain part-time or full-time clinical practices while they teach, allowing them to bring current clinical realities into the classroom.

Chiropractors who enter into education as a profession may also find that their institution will help them earn further academic degrees to enhance the quality of academic chiropractic. Educators also have the opportunity to present educational research and innovations at numerous conferences and symposia, furthering the education of chiropractors worldwide.

Research

Research is a vital part of chiropractic advancement, just as it is in all health-care professions, and it is a rewarding way to contribute to the advancement of the profession and general public welfare. The chiropractic researcher usually associates with an accredited chiropractic college, university, hospital, clinic, health and welfare organization, or private industry.

With the great need to conduct high-quality research, there are more chiropractic researchers than ever before. Opportunities exist for D.C.s to be trained in research methodology and theory and to pursue advanced academic degrees. Fellowship opportunities are also available to help aspiring researchers secure the funds necessary to achieve these goals. Increased federal funding for research related to chiropractic has reached an all-time high. Researchers now have opportunities to apply for numerous grants to fund specific projects and programs, and their research is presented at prestigious international conferences and regularly published in high-quality scientific journals.

The chiropractic profession is engaged in several research programs investigating the effectiveness and safety of chiropractic care. Basic science and clinical research is being done that investigates the relationship of the chiropractic subluxation to tissues in the spine and the rest of the body. Educational research is conducted to evaluate effective teaching and student assessment strategies. To review summaries of chiropractic research, visit the National Library of Medicine at the PubMed website (pubmed.com), the Foundation for Chiropractic Education and Research (fcer.org), and the World Federation of Chiropractic (wfc.org). Research and development have identified new areas of need for the doctor of chiropractic and will no doubt provide many more new opportunities in the future.

Preventive Health Care

The chiropractic profession focuses on prevention. Doctors of chiropractic receive extensive prevention training and are a highly appropriate resource to effectively intervene in matters of nutritional counseling, substance abuse education, weight control, smoking cessation, postural correction, workplace safety, stress management, repetitive motion injuries, and ergonomic design and injury prevention.

Americans lag far behind many countries of the world in physical fitness. Space-age developments have encouraged a lifestyle of minimal physical effort. Nature, however, is not wasteful. What is not used degenerates. Our physical fitness is no exception.

Since its development, the chiropractic profession has offered national and community leadership in encouraging parents and teachers to support physical fitness programs in schools. In homes, youngsters must be encouraged to develop good fitness and health habits at an early age. Fitness is a family affair.

When biomechanics are disturbed through stress and strain, distortion results because of the interrelationship of our structural and functional systems. Posture not only has a direct bearing on comfort and work efficiency, it is also a factor that determines resistance to disease and disability.

Chiropractic is attentive to the importance of nerve integrity and body mechanics for good health. The doctor of chiropractic is concerned with the effects and prevention of spinal defects affecting physical fitness. He or she is trained to treat many health problems, and this treatment is aimed at maintaining mechanical integrity by correcting spinal and extraspinal defects and postural distortions.

To ensure health, our bodies must be free from structural distortions and must operate at peak efficiency. Any activity in which the structure of the human frame is thrown out of normal balance can cause distortion of the spine, which not only supports the weight of the entire body above the pelvis but also protects the spinal cord.

The involvement of chiropractors in public health programs is growing at an astounding rate, allowing D.C.s to educate the public on matters of health promotion and disease prevention. As early as 1930, the White House Conference on Child Health recognized the importance of spinal integrity and body mechanics in relation to health. Correct posture is essential to proper development, balance, coordination, rhythm, and timing. There is an undisputed relationship between good posture and good health. Chiropractors work toward the betterment of the nation's health. There is a special Chiropractic Health Care section in the American Public Health Association (APHA) dedicated to promoting better health through chiropractic services and finding ways for chiropractors to become involved in national public health agendas. You can visit this section of the APHA on the Internet (c3r.org/chirohealth).

Women and Minorities in Chiropractic

There is a great need for women and minorities in the chiropractic profession. Research performed by the National Board of Chiropractic Examiners estimates that approximately 20 percent of practicing chiropractors are women. This figure is up from research reported in 1993, when women comprised about 13 percent of the profession. (Christensen et al., 2000)

The number of non-Caucasian chiropractors is growing, but the chiropractic profession needs greater diversity. In 1998 the National Boards estimated that Asian, African-American, Hispanic, Native American, and other ethnicities made up 6.5 percent of practicing chiropractors. Although this number was greater than the 4.3 percent reported in 1993, there is still more work that needs to be done to reach out to these communities.

Chiropractic Abroad

Legislation licensing the practice of chiropractic exists in all U.S. states, the Canadian provinces, Mexico, and numerous other countries abroad. A list of contact information is provided in Appendix

A. Each year more countries continue to pass laws and legislation providing licensure for chiropractors, and this trend is expected to continue. The World Federation of Chiropractic keeps a close watch on worldwide legislation, and its website (wfc.org) provides the most current information. Common features in most of these jurisdictions are: primary care (direct contact with patient), the right and duty to diagnose, and the right to use diagnostic x-ray.

Major chiropractic colleges exist in the United States (17) and Canada (2) as well as many other countries. A list of colleges and contact information is provided in Appendix B. In the United States, chiropractic colleges are typically private. An exception to this rule is the University of Bridgeport Chiropractic College, where chiropractic education is provided within a university setting. The university model is the model of preference in other countries, including Denmark, Australia, Brazil, and the United Kingdom. A number of European countries, such as the Scandinavian countries, require returning graduates to meet formal postgraduate requirements.

Chiropractic Outreach Programs

Numerous programs are currently available for chiropractic students and doctors to provide chiropractic care to underserved areas of the United States and other countries. Chiropractors routinely provide health care services for thousands of people in foreign lands where people have never been exposed to chiropractic.

The Christian Chiropractors Association places world missions at the heart of its program. The association sends chiropractic missionaries into Belize, Bolivia, Brazil, Colombia, Cuba, Ecuador, Haiti, Hungary, Jamaica, Kenya, Mexico, Peru, Poland, and the

Ukraine. Missions also go to various Native American Indian tribes. To find out more, visit christianchiropractors.org.

Several chiropractic colleges also offer approved educational programs for chiropractic interns to provide care to various communities under the direct supervision of chiropractic college faculty. These programs are very rewarding for students, providing opportunities to manage patients with a variety of health care needs. Locally, programs are often at various inner-city locations, HIV treatment centers, Salvation Army and Goodwill facilities, and other such locations. Interns often may choose to travel to Indian reservations, other states, and even out of the country to participate in these programs. For more information, ask the representatives of the colleges that you are considering.

4

A Day in the Life of a Chiropractor

Chiropractic is a desirable profession with great career potential. The profession advocates a holistic, natural approach to health care and emphasizes staying healthy rather than viewing health as the absence of illness. Chiropractors adjust the joints of the body to correct subluxations and help patients heal. But, just what is it that chiropractors do? Perhaps the best way to understand this is to spend a day in the life of a chiropractor.

Typical Workday

Many chiropractors work their longest hours on Monday, Wednesday, and Friday and are open from 7:00 A.M. to noon and 2:00 to 6:00 P.M. Often the office may be open for only half a day on Tuesday, Thursday, and Saturday. These are typical office hours, but serving patients' needs, local demographics, and location of the office influence office hours. Most D.C.s do not work on Sundays,

53

except for occasional emergencies. Chiropractors start their days early because many patients like to be seen before work. About half of D.C.s report working thirty to thirty-nine hours per week. The typical doctor of chiropractic practices 4.2 days each week, in which he or she attends to the needs of an average of 116 patient visits. (Christensen et al., 2000)

Since most chiropractors are independent and operate their own businesses, the day usually starts with typical duties such as unlocking the doors and preparing the office for patients. Most D.C.s also review reports and new information on patients, review the daily schedule, catch up on reading professional news or journals, and verify that the equipment they will need for the day is ready.

Like many professionals, a long lunch period allows time for the chiropractor to attend civic functions, meet with community leaders, and hold staff meetings, which accounts for about 15 percent of their time. Chiropractors report that on average about half of their time is spent on direct patient care, 20 percent on business management and practice promotion, and about 15 percent on paperwork and documentation. The chiropractor usually employs some office staff to help with patient care, promote the practice, greet and process patients, prepare paperwork, and do the billing. As manager of his or her business, the D.C. must have good team-building skills.

Patient Care

Chiropractors see two types of patients: those who are returning for care, and those who are new to the practice. Each type of encounter is described here to provide the reader with a better idea of what chiropractors offer their patients.

Returning Patients Who Are Healthy

Most morning patients are regular visitors to the D.C.'s office who usually see the doctor for periodic spinal adjustments and counseling on health-promoting activities such as diet, exercise, and stress relief. A typical appointment begins with the D.C. asking the patient a series of brief questions to check his or her health status and to verify that the patient is making progress toward his or her health goal. Since this patient has been managed by the chiropractor for some time, a complete physical examination is not necessary each time the patient visits the office.

Some patients have no specific complaint and come to the office for a periodic spinal adjustment to maintain good spinal biomechanics. For these patients, the D.C. will perform a brief examination of the spine to determine how to best adjust the patient. A periodic spinal examination usually includes an analysis of the patient's walk and posture to look for any abnormalities that can indicate spinal dysfunction. The D.C. will also observe the patient's back to look for areas of tight muscles, asymmetrical form, and skin discoloration.

Chiropractors will then spend time palpating, or evaluating by the use of touch, the patient's spine. During palpation, the D.C. assesses the health of the skin, checks for tenderness in the muscles and joints, and evaluates the movement of the spine. Chiropractors will also evaluate the quality and quantity of spinal motion and perform other standard diagnostic procedures as necessary.

Chiropractors will also include in their patient analysis one or more procedures that aid in identifying the location and type of subluxation present. Most of these procedures are part of what chiropractors call "technique systems." A technique system is a particular way of analyzing and adjusting a chiropractic subluxation. Analytical methods include the use of palpation, range of motion and spinal biomechanical evaluation, muscle testing, observation of reflexes, skin temperature instrumentation, and a variety of other observations. Patients will not undergo x-rays on routine visits to the chiropractor; x-rays are taken only when necessary.

Once the chiropractor has determined that a subluxation is present, he or she will adjust it. When performing an adjustment, the D.C. delivers a highly controlled, specific, quick thrust to the joint that he or she has determined is subluxated. Chiropractors spend years training in this art and concentrate a great deal of their education on perfecting the delivery of a proper adjustment.

The D.C. most commonly uses his or her hands to deliver an adjustment. However, some techniques use various mechanical instruments to give the adjustment. When giving an adjustment, the chiropractor will apply gentle traction to the joint to enable a comfortable adjustment. When he or she can feel that the joint is positioned correctly for the adjustment, a gentle thrust is delivered to the joint. Almost all adjustments are painless and most patients enjoy being adjusted. It is not uncommon for patients to remark that they did not know how tense or tight they were in a particular area of their body until after being adjusted, when that area seems more relaxed and mobile.

Adjustments may be performed on any of the joints of the body. As mentioned before, there are numerous adjusting methods, or techniques, used today. The most popular technique is called diversified technique, which represents a portfolio of the most common adjusting procedures taught in chiropractic colleges. Over 95 percent of chiropractors use diversified technique in their offices. (Christensen et al., 2000)

Sometimes the term "manipulation" is used to describe what chiropractors do with their hands when they adjust a patient. The chiropractor's repertoire includes all forms of manual therapy: massage, mobilization, and various forms of manipulation. However, the term manipulation has been used loosely in the past, often to refer to all manual techniques used to treat muscles or joints. During the past few decades the following definitions have become distinct in the United States and international health science literature with respect to treatment of joint disorders:

- **Massage.** Manual treatment directed primarily at the soft tissues (ligaments, muscles, fascia) of the body.
- **Mobilization.** Slower (low-velocity) techniques in which the joint remains within its passive range of movement. The treatment can be monitored and resisted by the patient, who therefore has final control.
- **Manipulation.** Faster (high-velocity) techniques that take the joint beyond the passive range end barrier to what is known as the "paraphysiological" space. The skilled doctor often thereby intentionally increases range of movement of the joint. Because of the faster speed involved, the patient does not have complete control of the process. Therefore, potential for harm in unskilled hands is greater.
- **Adjustment.** The chiropractic adjustment is a highly skilled and specific form of manipulation. Chiropractors receive more training in this form of care than any other health-care provider and provide an adjustment with the intention of normalizing joint function and improving neurological function. For these reasons, many chiropractors prefer to use the term "adjustment" instead of "manipulation."

Chiropractic adjusting techniques are remarkably safe procedures. There are fewer risks associated with chiropractic care than most other interventions. This is the primary reason why malpractice insurance premium rates are so low for chiropractors. The malpractice premiums that a chiropractor pays can vary from state to state with the national average, but they cost approximately $1,200. This stands in sharp comparison with the average national premium ranging from $6,000 to $12,000 for malpractice insurance of a general practice medical doctor. A study from the RAND Corporation indicates that over 90 percent of manipulative services provided in the United States are given by the chiropractic profession. (Coulter et al., 1996)

Chiropractors provide additional care for their patients. Chiropractors will often use ice or heat before or after an adjustment. Most D.C.s will employ some type of procedure to address muscular problems. Some of these procedures are also done by hand and involve manual compression or deep massage of irritated muscular tissue. Some D.C.s may utilize other physiotherapeutic modalities, such as electrical stimulation, ultrasound, and hydrotherapy.

All of the procedures described above are passive, meaning that the doctor does these for the patient. However, chiropractors are strong advocates for active care, and over 90 percent of D.C.s report incorporating one or more active care strategies in their practice. Active care involves patient education, and chiropractors spend about 15 percent of their time providing patient and community education. Chiropractors try to help their patients learn how to better care for themselves to prevent disease and promote a healthy lifestyle. Most commonly, D.C.s make recommendations regarding diet, exercise, correct posture, and work biomechanics. In addition, chiropractors will encourage their patients to stop smoking, limit alcohol consumption, use good hygiene, and engage in other health-promoting behaviors.

Returning Patients Who Have a Current Problem

Many returning patients are those who initially seek chiropractic care because they have an ailment or accident that causes them pain or dysfunction. In fact, most patients come to chiropractic care initially seeking pain relief or restoration of function and only then realize that chiropractic care is of great benefit in maintaining a healthy lifestyle. The typical office visit for these patients is usually focused on their current problem.

After taking a brief history from the patient to determine the progress of the complaint, the chiropractor will briefly examine the area of concern to check its progress and then determine an appropriate course of care for that day. Since this patient would have recently received a comprehensive examination when he or she initially came to the office for help, a complete physical examination is not necessary at this time.

When patients have a primary complaint, the chiropractor focuses his or her energy on helping the patient's body heal the problem as quickly as possible. Therapy is initially aimed at minimizing pain and beginning to restore function to the injured area. Like healthy patients described above, chiropractors will adjust areas that are in need. Chiropractors do not prescribe drugs and do not perform surgery. If such therapies are needed, the D.C. will make a referral to the appropriate health-care provider and co-manage the patient using chiropractic methods.

Therapeutic methods in chiropractic are numerous and are usually targeted at supporting the healing tissues and the nervous system. Chiropractors are trained in first aid and may have to provide it for acute injuries. Joints that have too much motion are often rehabilitated using a progressive rehabilitation program. First, the joints are typically supported using braces, tape, or straps, and exercises are begun to support the injured area. Later, more aggressive muscle strengthening and coordination exercises are added to the patient management plan.

The D.C. may also recommend some dietary regimens and nutritional supplements that are designed to prevent the onset or lessen the existence of some types of dysfunction of the nervous system and other tissues. Physiotherapeutic modalities are frequently used as adjunctive therapy to enhance both the reception and the effects of chiropractic adjustments. Such procedures may include traction, diathermy, galvanic currents, infrared and ultraviolet light, ultrasound, massage, paraffin baths, hot or cold compresses or baths, acupressure, heel or sole shoe lifts, foot stabilizers, and other modalities.

Once a patient is out of an acutely painful state, the D.C. will begin to focus the patient's attention on returning to optimum function. Changes in the management plan will be made and the chiropractor will begin training the patient in self-care. The patient will progress through a few stages of management until his or her problem is resolved. Prior to resolution, most chiropractors talk to their patients about the need for periodic chiropractic care and consultation to lead a healthier life.

New Patients

When a patient first comes to a chiropractor, he or she will be given a comprehensive consultation and examination. Additionally, the patient will usually complete a questionnaire, usually called a review of systems, to document the current and past health history of all of his or her body systems.

Once paperwork is complete, the chiropractor will interview the patient to discover his or her needs and ask questions to better understand the patient's complaint. During the initial patient interview and consultation, every measure of observation that substantially profiles the patient is employed and recorded. In addition to information about the patient's chief complaint, the D.C. will ask numerous questions about the patient's work and recreational habits, diet, exercise, and lifestyle to obtain a complete picture of the patient's health. At the completion of the interview, the chiropractor forms a list of potential diagnoses that he or she will rule in or out during the examination process. As is standard in health care, all information pertaining to the patient is kept strictly confidential.

Following the interview is a thorough examination. The D.C. will measure the patient's vital signs, height, and weight. In addition to an examination focused on the problem area, most chiropractors will also perform a complete physical examination on the patient so that the patient's total health is assessed. All current physical, orthopedic, and neurological testing is performed to best determine what structures are in need of chiropractic care, or if the patient needs to be referred to another health-care provider. The chiropractor will also perform a complete spinal analysis, including evaluation of the patient's gait, posture, movement, and biomechanics. Analysis of the patient's spine for subluxation is performed and all information is recorded in the patient's file.

When the examination is complete, the chiropractor may take x-rays, also called radiographs, of the area of concern. Radiographs are not mandatory; guidelines for taking x-rays are used to determine if they are necessary. Due to costs of operating equipment, increasing numbers of doctors of chiropractic elect not to have x-ray equipment in their own office, but rather have clinical arrangements with freestanding diagnostic facilities or hospital x-ray facilities. In some instances, the D.C. may wish to order further tests, such as blood or urine laboratory tests or advanced diagnostic imaging.

Once all of the information about the patient is obtained, the chiropractor will establish a diagnosis of the patient's condition and develop an appropriate management plan. The management plan will take the patient's unique situation in mind and usually consists of a trial period of adjustments and other forms of care. During this trial period, the D.C. will keep careful notes on the patient's progress and modify the management plan accordingly.

Prior to initiating care, the doctor will provide a report to the patient of the findings of the history and examination and present the suggested management plan. For patients new to chiropractic, the doctor usually provides a brief explanation of the profession and management procedures to fully inform the patient of his or her care. At this time most chiropractors will educate the patient about the benefits and risks of chiropractic care and of the various other treatment options and will obtain consent from the patient prior to beginning care. Chiropractors spend a great deal of time communicating with their patients, which is one reason why chiropractic patients in so many studies have indicated a high degree of satisfaction. Following the report of findings, the management plan begins. Then the patient is considered a returning patient, until his or her health status changes.

Work Conditions

The work conditions of chiropractors are an important aspect of the appeal of chiropractic practice. This section describes the chiropractic office environment for those who may not be familiar with this exciting environment.

Office Environment

The chiropractic office is a pleasant environment. Most chiropractors design their offices to be comfortable, patient friendly, clean, relaxing, and quiet, which is conducive to patients' relaxation and healing. Since chiropractors deal with ambulatory patients, they do not have to work with blood and other body fluids, such as in an emergency department. Most patients are happy and look forward to being in the office. For these, and other reasons, chiropractic has been selected as one of the top ten careers for jobs requiring a professional degree. (jist.com)

Office Layout

A chiropractor's office usually has a front desk area where the receptionist greets patients and where active patient files are kept. There is a reception room and many D.C.s place educational materials there for patients to read or view while they wait. Usually there is one or more examination rooms, a room for taking x-rays, a room for processing x-ray films, and one or more rooms for providing chiropractic care, often called treatment rooms. It is necessary to have separate treatment rooms because chiropractors use special tables for performing chiropractic adjustments. (Tables used in examination rooms are usually taller than those used for adjusting patients.) Many chiropractors will also have an area designated for rehabilitation equipment and physiotherapeutic modalities. Usually the doctor keeps a private office, where he or she conducts personal business, although some D.C.s like to use these offices for the initial patient interview and report of findings as well.

Typical Patients

The chiropractor sees a variety of patients during the day. The National Board of Chiropractic Examiners reports that a little more than half of chiropractic patients are women. (Christensen et al., 2000) About 16 percent of chiropractic patients are under seventeen years of age, 34 percent are over the age of fifty, and about half are between the ages of eighteen and fifty. The chiropractic patient population is diverse, including approximately 14 percent Hispanics, 13 percent African-Americans, 8 percent Asian/Pacific Islander, and 5 percent Native American. Caucasians make up about 60 percent of chiropractic patients.

Many people think that chiropractors see primarily blue-collar workers because these people often have back pain. It is true that many of these workers use chiropractic care, making up about 35 percent of patients. However, 37 percent of workers who seek chiropractic services are those who work in white-collar occupations, including administrative and clerical support, executives and managers, educators, sales representatives, and those in technical fields. The remainder is made up of athletes, entertainers, home workers, and retired people who bring their unique needs to the chiropractic encounter.

Personal Attributes

Several personal attributes are important in the practice of chiropractic. Doctors must be able to physically perform the duties of chiropractic, understand and communicate with their patients and community, and engage in continuing education.

Characteristics

The typical doctor is married, Caucasian, and male. Approximately 20 percent of American chiropractors are female. (Christensen et al., 2000) The average chiropractor is thirty-seven years of age and has a 50 percent chance of living in a city with a population of more than fifty thousand. The average D.C. has been in practice between ten and fifteen years. However, there are a great number of chiropractors who enjoy their careers to such a degree that they never fully retire and stay involved in patient care or professional duties for thirty years or more. Chiropractors are actively involved in postgraduate education to stay abreast of recent advancements in the field. All states have continuing education requirements, but many D.C.s exceed these requirements by attending several courses and by self-study.

Physical Fitness

Providing chiropractic care takes physical and mental energy, but the energy expenditure is returned tenfold when the D.C. witnesses patients improving under his or her care. It takes a certain degree of strength and endurance to be on your feet all day seeing to the needs of patients. For this reason, it is recommended that the chiropractor stay in good physical condition. Additionally, a healthy chiropractor serves as a role model for his or her patients and possesses more credibility when speaking with patients about matters of good health.

Communication Skills

Since the chiropractor is the leader in his or her office, good communication skills are a necessity. The D.C. must have excellent personal interaction skills, since he or she interacts not only with patients, but the office staff, insurance companies, other chiropractors, the community, and other health-care providers. It is essential that the D.C. have good public speaking skills as well, because he or she will provide group presentations in addition to speaking with people personally.

Conditions Treated

The three most common reasons that new patients seek chiropractic care are for the relief of low-back pain, neck pain, and headache or facial pain. A recent study reported that approximately 20 percent of patients with neck or back pain saw chiropractors for relief. (Wolsko et al., 2003) Problems of the middle back and extremities are the next most common reasons, and about 12 percent of symptomatic patients seek chiropractic care for the relief of disorders that are not musculoskeletal in nature.

Low-Back Pain

Low-back and pelvic pain and injury comprise about 25 percent of chiropractic cases. Although this number may seem small to some, low-back pain accounts for the single largest percentage of workers' compensation benefit payments and injury. Spinal manipulation has become one of the more extensively studied treatments, including more than forty experimental research studies known as randomized clinical trials. (Meeker and Haldeman, 2002)

Even though such compelling evidence exists regarding the relationship of chiropractic care and low-back pain, it must be acknowledged that there are still far more questions than answers in the health sciences, even in the area of treatment for low-back problems. For example, the various biological mechanisms that cause most back pain problems remain unknown. Once scientists have a better idea of what causes low-back pain, we will presumably be able to invent better methods of preventing and more permanently overcoming this ubiquitous disorder.

An economic study suggests that millions of dollars can be saved by transferring the management of low-back pain to chiropractors.

(Manga et al., 1993) Widely known as the Manga Report, named after health economist Pran Manga, Ph.D., its conclusions are nothing short of remarkable in their support of chiropractic for the care of low-back pain. Funded by the Ontario Ministry of Health, the Manga Report strongly supports the effectiveness and cost-effectiveness of chiropractic spinal manipulation over surgery, bed rest, and various physical therapy procedures and modalities in treating low-back pain. This report is available on the Internet (chiropractic.on.ca).

The Manga Report offered evidence and expert testimony from Australia, Canada, the United Kingdom, and the United States of potential savings of many millions of dollars annually if more of the management of low-back pain was in fact transferred from medical doctors to chiropractors. This report also stated that spinal manipulation applied by chiropractors is shown to be more effective and safer than other treatments for low-back pain. Simply put, despite economic disincentives for use of chiropractic services, chiropractic has met the market test of consumer choice and preference.

Dr. Manga also suggested that research offers an overwhelming case in favor of much greater use of chiropractic services for the management of low-back pain. He also recommended that hospital privileges should be extended to all chiropractors for the purposes of treatment of their own patients who have been hospitalized for other reasons, and for access to diagnostic facilities relevant to their scope of practice and patients' needs.

Neck Pain and Headache

Patients with neck pain and headache comprise approximately 20 and 13 percent, respectively, of symptomatic chiropractic patients.

Several research studies demonstrate that the care chiropractors provide is effective in managing various kinds of neck disorders. Spinal manipulation by itself has demonstrated effectiveness in alleviating neck pain and is perhaps even more effective than mobilization or physical therapy. (Hurwitz et al., 1996; Coulter et al., 1996)

In 2003, researchers in the Netherlands reported that spinal mobilization was more effective and less costly for treating neck pain than physiotherapy or care by a general medical practitioner. (Korthals-de Bos et al., 2003) Another recent study revealed that chiropractic adjustments combined with rehabilitation programs may be the most effective approach to combating this problem. (Evans et al., 2002)

Patients suffering from various kinds of headache often report relief from chiropractic care. The type of headache researched most by chiropractors is called cervicogenic headache, meaning that head pain is caused by problems in the upper neck. Cervicogenic headache responds well to chiropractic care, as several research studies have demonstrated. A recent review of several scientific studies revealed that spinal manipulation had a better effect than massage for cervicogenic headaches. In the same study, spinal manipulation had comparable outcomes to first-line prescription medications for other migraine and tension headaches. (Bronfort et al., 2001) Further research into the effectiveness of chiropractic care for this and other headache types is ongoing.

Some have voiced concern regarding the safety of spinal manipulation of the neck. It is difficult to estimate the risk of complications following a chiropractic adjustment to the neck for several reasons. One reason for this is that numerous times these accidents have been reported as "chiropractic treatments," even though the treatments were not actually performed by a chiropractor. A prominent doctor from Australia, Dr. Allan Terrett, demonstrated that many such reported "chiropractic treatments" were actually performed by masseurs, physical therapists, naturopaths, medical doctors, and a variety of other nonchiropractors. (Terrett, 1995) Thus, in many reports suggesting that chiropractic adjustments are harmful, the procedure was not performed by a chiropractor.

The risk of complication following cervical manipulation is very difficult to predict because so few accidents have actually been reported. The best estimates suggest that the risk of a certain type of stroke is one in four hundred thousand to between three and six per ten million manipulations. (Meeker and Haldeman, 2002) Comparatively, one in a thousand patients who take nonsteroidal anti-inflammatory medications suffer a serious gastrointestinal problem leading to hospitalization or death. (Coulter et al., 1996) Like any procedure, the chiropractor must weigh the potential benefits and risks before using cervical manipulation. Chiropractors are trained to screen their patients for known risk factors during the examination; however, it is impossible to predict if a patient will have a side effect from an adjustment because many problems occur without the provocation of an adjustment. For example, some people have been known to have a stroke simply from turning their head to look over their shoulder while driving. More research is being done to determine risks of cervical manipulation.

Other Disorders

Beyond the three disorders just discussed, there is a need for research into a variety of other health-care problems and their appropriate management. Various studies are published documenting chiropractic approaches to problems with the upper and lower extremities. For more than a century, beginning with chiropractic's first patient, Harvey Lillard and his hearing problem, D.C.s have offered service to patients for a wide range of clinical problems; these treatments have been based on the apparent benefits that patients report back to their chiropractic doctors. Among the diseases for which a benefit of chiropractic care has been suggested are asthma, colic, menstrual pain, chronic pelvic pain, ulcers, high blood pressure, and various nervous and mental disorders.

Chiropractic is just entering a progressive age of discovery to document potentially beneficial approaches to managing such human ailments. The growth in chiropractic research in recent decades bespeaks a greater concern among D.C.s for the proper use of science. Many chiropractors have grown more cautious in the claims they make for the value of their healing art. They recognize that respect within the health-science community and the wider public depends upon a willingness to distinguish that which is known with confidence from that which is still speculative.

This healthy, self-generated caution and skepticism does not mean abandonment of hypotheses before they have been tested, but rather a resistance to making claims for methods and theories that have not yet been adequately tested. If you are interested in knowing more about the status of chiropractic research, visit the website of the Foundation for Chiropractic Education and Research (fcer.org) or contact the National Chiropractic Board of Examiners and ask for a pamphlet that summarizes studies related to chiropractic.

Like all doctors, chiropractors will continue to provide the best available assessment and treatment methods, even when the best possible information has not yet been developed. Physicians of all schools, be they chiropractic, osteopathic, or medical, will attempt to meet their patient needs based upon their education in the basic sciences, their supervised clinical training, their accumulated clinical wisdom, and, when available, hard scientific data.

Wellness

Both in philosophy and practice, chiropractors advocate a healthy lifestyle. The National Board of Chiropractic Examiners reports that almost 10 percent of patients see chiropractors for wellness and preventive care. To work with a patient to stay healthy, resolve problems before they become crises, and develop health-promoting lifestyles makes good sense. Certainly many people think that they are healthy as long as they do not have a symptom, disease, or other illness. However, when one waits to develop a symptom, it is often a late manifestation of a problem that has been going on for some time. Chiropractors like to help patients prevent such problems by teaching them how to eat, sleep, play, and work safely.

A recent study demonstrated that the majority of chiropractors employ a variety of health promotion and disease prevention strategies in their practices, including exercise, proper eating habits, and patient education regarding alcohol, smoking, and drug use. The majority of chiropractors also viewed chiropractic adjustments as important components of maintenance care. In contrast to the National Boards data, the D.C.s in this study estimated that about 34 percent of patient visits are for the purpose of health-promoting activities, generating an estimated 23 percent of the responding chiropractors' revenue. (Rupert, 2000)

In another study, the same author and a team of additional researchers found that for patients sixty-five years of age and older, in addition to periodic adjustments, chiropractors recommended stretching exercises, cardiovascular exercises, and general diet advice for 68.2, 55.6, and 45.3 percent, respectively, of their patients. The patients in this study reported using both chiropractic and medical care, but they made half of the annual number of visits to medical doctors compared to people in the same age group on a national average. This reduction in cost, due to a lesser need for hospitalization and other medical services for these patients, was estimated to be one-third of the national average for patients of the same age. (Rupert et al., 2000)

Duties Outside of the Practice

The typical chiropractor is an active and contributing member of local community and civic groups. The doctor has a position of responsibility to patients and community and uses professional abilities conscientiously and with integrity to serve those who depend upon her or him for proper health care and advice. Chiropractors often donate their services at community and athletic events, at facilities for underserved communities, and at other functions. Many chiropractors are involved in professional organizations or specialty groups. Various organizations and associations may be found in Appendix A.

Being involved in service activities is rewarding and makes one well respected in his or her community. Many D.C.s are so involved in activities outside of their practice that they find that chiropractic permeates their life in a very positive way. Of course, the D.C. cannot involve himself or herself in such activities only during office hours. Such devotion requires service to be done in between patients, during special appointments, at lunch, and before and after regular work hours. Therefore, the end of a chiropractor's day may often include activities that support his or her service to the community or profession.

Visiting a Chiropractor

The best way to understand the daily activities of a chiropractor is to simply go and visit with one during a typical day. Many people thinking of going into chiropractic as a profession are chiropractic patients. However, understanding the chiropractic professional life from the viewpoint of a patient is different than actually seeing what happens during the course of an entire day.

To find a D.C. to visit, call some of the colleges that you are thinking of attending and ask for the names of some alumni in your area. Call these doctors and tell them you are considering becoming a chiropractor. Always make an appointment before you visit, so that the doctor can make time to speak with you as well as any other arrangements that may be necessary. Most D.C.s are excited to share their experiences with prospective students, and you will more than likely find that the D.C. is a consummate host. Since there are a variety of chiropractic techniques, you may wish to visit a few different chiropractors to get a broader view of the profession.

Before you visit a D.C., you will want to have some questions ready to help you better understand chiropractic. Here is a list of potential questions to consider:

What is the most exciting thing about being a chiropractor?
How long is your typical workday or workweek?
What is the most difficult thing about being a
    chiropractor?
What chiropractic college did you attend?
What chiropractic colleges do you recommend?
Do you have enough time to spend with your family and
    do other things that you like to do?
What chiropractic techniques do you use? Why?
Why did you become a chiropractor?
What are some of the most exciting patient cases that you
    have seen?
What recommendations do you have for making it through
    chiropractic college?

There are some general guidelines that you should follow when you visit a chiropractor. Always dress professionally. You are entering a professional office, and you will want to look the part. Ask the doctor ahead of time if there are any general times that he or she would prefer that you do not talk. It is very important for the doctor to give patients his or her undivided attention. Therefore, the D.C. may ask you to write your questions down and ask them later. Ask the D.C. where you should sit during various situations so that you can watch what is happening, but not be in the way. Due to patient privacy, there will be times when you may not be permitted to watch a patient encounter. If you are asked not to be present, do not feel rejected. Simply understand that the chiropractor is respecting patient rights. After your office visit, it is customary to send the doctor and his or her staff a card indicating your appreciation.

5

EDUCATIONAL PREPARATION FOR CHIROPRACTIC COLLEGE

ONCE YOU HAVE made the decision to become a chiropractor, you must turn your attention to preparing for and selecting an institution of higher learning. This chapter will help you with all the steps involved in this important process.

Admissions

The admissions requirements for chiropractic college are similar to those for other health-care fields. Selection for matriculation is typically based upon grade point average and the possession of specific undergraduate course units. Although not all colleges require a bachelor's degree for entrance, there is a trend toward increasing entrance requirements to this level.

Required Units

The typical applicant at a chiropractic college has already acquired nearly four years of premedical undergraduate college education, including courses in biology, inorganic and organic chemistry, physics, psychology, and related lab work. All recognized U.S. chiropractic colleges require applicants to have at least two years of ninety acceptable semester hours leading to a baccalaureate degree in the arts and sciences from an institution accredited by a nationally recognized agency. Preprofessional credits must be earned at institutions listed in the *Education Directory—Higher Education of the U.S. Department of Education*. Applicants must be graduates of or eligible to return to the last institution attended.

For admission beginning with the fall class of 2003, the ninety-hour minimum also had to include at least thirty hours of upper-division credit. In addition, all matriculants must have had earned a cumulative grade point average of a minimum of 2.50 on a scale of 4.00 for the required prerequisite courses. As mentioned above, the trend in educational requirements from various state licensing bodies as well as demands from within the profession leans toward requiring a baccalaureate degree prior to entrance to chiropractic college. Students should verify this requirement before making the decision in which state to practice. One college currently requires a baccalaureate degree as an entrance requirement and others will undoubtedly follow. Thus, not all colleges require a bachelor's degree for entrance, although more colleges are working toward this requirement.

Additionally, all students must have a minimum of forty-eight semester hour credits, distributed as follows:

- English Language Skills—6 semester hours
- Psychology—3 semester hours
- Social Sciences or Humanities—15 semester hours
- Biological Sciences—6 semester hours
- Chemistry—12 semester hours
- Physics and related studies—6 semester hours

Quarter-hour credits may be converted to equivalent semester hour credits.

In situations in which one or more courses have been repeated with equivalent courses, the most recent grade(s) may be used for grade point average computation and the earlier grade(s) may be disregarded. No more than twenty semester hours of a candidate's preprofessional education may be acquired through CLEP (College Level Examination Program) examinations.

Candidate Attributes

Chiropractic requires keen observational skills to detect physical abnormalities and the signs of health attributes of patients. It also takes considerable dexterity and coordination to perform adjustments. Chiropractors work independently and, therefore, must demonstrate responsibility and efficiency. As in other health-related occupations, empathy, understanding, and the desire to help others are important qualities for effectively managing patients.

Personal qualifications for those considering a chiropractic career should include: above-average mental ability, ability to manage time and work independently, a strong desire to serve the sick, ability to maintain high ethical and professional standards, tact, patience, adaptability, ability to inspire confidence and respect, high moral character and integrity, and manual skill and dexterity.

The Personal Interview

All applicants should expect to have a personal interview at the colleges where they are applying. Even if a student's grades are high and he or she has the best references, that student should expect an interview since all students are in competition for a place in an entering class. Although the interviewers will attempt to put the student at ease, the prospective applicant should think about some of the possible questions that the interviewers might ask and outline what might be said.

Sample interview questions may include the following:

Why do you want to be a doctor of chiropractic?
How much contact have you had with chiropractic?
What do you know about chiropractic?
Are you interested in science?
How do you plan to successfully complete the program at
    this college?
What are your plans to finance your education?
How do you feel about working with sick people?

Transfer of Credits and Advanced Standing

Students who wish to transfer from one chiropractic college to another must meet the admission requirements of the transferee institution at the time of the students' original matriculation. Such students must present the institution to be entered with a letter of recommendation from the transfer institution, and the students' transfer credits must be identifiable to the curriculum of the trans-feree institution.

Credits considered for transfer to a chiropractic college must have been awarded for courses taken in a program accredited by the Council on Chiropractic Education (CCE). An exception to this would be if a student wished to transfer credits earned from a first professional health sciences degree or graduate program (for example, M.D. or D.O.). Such credits must be earned at an institution that is recognized by a national accrediting agency. Only credits on an official transcript with an equivalent grade of 2.00 on a 4.00 scale or better may be transferred. In addition, transferred credits cannot be used for double credit; that is, they cannot be used to meet both prechiropractic and chiropractic requirements.

Transfer credits must be formally evaluated by the receiving program to be substantially equivalent to courses offered by the receiving program in the D.C. curriculum. Credits accepted for transfer must have been awarded within five years of the date of admission to the receiving program. Transfer credits from institutions outside the United States must be accompanied by evidence of the student's proficiency in the subject matter of each course for which credits are considered.

When students have interrupted their chiropractic training for a period in excess of five years, credit is not allowed upon re-enrollment or transfer for courses previously taken. Such a student must also meet current admission requirements.

Applicants for admission to advanced standing are required to furnish evidence that:

1. They can meet the same entrance requirements as candidates for the first-year class

2. Courses equivalent in content and quality to those given in the admitting college in the year or years preceding that to which admission is desired have been satisfactorily completed
3. The work was done in a chiropractic college acceptable to the committee on admissions of the college
4. The candidate has a letter of recommendation from the dean of the college from which transfer is made

Credits for work done in accredited colleges of liberal arts and sciences will be allowed only in nonclinical subjects. However, applicable credit may be granted to an applicant who has taken professional clinical work in an accredited medical or osteopathic college. No candidate will be accepted from such colleges if dishonorably dismissed.

For all students admitted to advanced standing, the college entered is required to have on file with the registrar:

1. The same documents that are required for admission to the first-year class
2. A certified transcript of work completed
3. A letter indicating honorable withdrawal from the college from which the transfer was made

Foreign Students

To be admitted to a recognized chiropractic college within the United States, students who are not U.S. citizens must:

- Have the endorsement of the chiropractic organization of her or his home country, if such an organization exists.

- Submit proof of proficiency in the English language. A common method of establishing proficiency in English is through testing by the Institution for International Education or the U.S. State Department.
- Submit evidence of having the financial resources, or funding commitment, to complete a minimum of one year of education.
- Meet the same educational requirements as a student matriculating from the United States.
- Have the transcript evaluated by a CCE-designated agency. An official copy of the evaluation will be forwarded directly to the institution and the student.
- Meet the requirements that the U.S. government requires for foreign students.

Handicapped Students

Handicapped students are treated no differently from other students. They are not denied admission because of their handicap, nor are there any special scholastic requirements. On the other hand, special scholastic or other types of privileges need to be considered. For example, visually handicapped students will be required to carry out reading assignments and laboratory assignments as well as microscopic work and radiological interpretation.

Thus one should consider if his or her impairment might create insurmountable problems that can be anticipated before considering enrollment. Additional consideration for students with a physical handicap is whether they will be able to administer treatment to patients, the vast majority of whom will present with neuromusculoskeletal problems. Some handicaps may require an alteration in chiropractic technique and/or special equipment needs, which may add to the cost of equipment.

A handicap may, in fact, prove to be a positive attribute and enable the new graduate to provide services in a niche that may not have adequate chiropractic services. The decision regarding handicap enrollment is a very personal choice, and many practitioners with handicaps have enjoyed marvelous careers as doctors of chiropractic.

Selecting a Chiropractic College

One of the most important decisions for the prospective student is the selection of the college. The many years of training at the institution you attend will help you to develop the professional relationships necessary for your success and to construct the foundation from which you will launch your career. The type and style of education will determine who you become, so it is important to choose wisely when selecting a college.

Accreditation

To become licensed to practice, it is important to consider attending a college that is accredited by the CCE. The CCE and its Commission on Accreditation are recognized by the U.S. Department of Education as the sole reliable authority on the quality of training offered by chiropractic colleges. The CCE is a member of the Council of Specialized Accrediting Agencies (CSAA), an autonomous, nongovernmental accreditation agency. CSAA fosters the maintenance of high standards within the wide spectrum of postsecondary education.

Certain requirements must be met before a chiropractic college is considered for accreditation. Prescriptions that are set by the CCE require standard curricular content, specific faculty qualifications, faculty-student ratios, library holdings, and physical plant, school governance, administration, financial stability, and specific student entrance requirements. The reason that institutional accreditation by an institutional accrediting body is important is that this certifies to the general public that the institution: has appropriate purposes, has the resources needed to accomplish its purposes, can demonstrate that it is accomplishing its purposes, and gives reason to believe that it will continue to accomplish its purposes.

The CCE periodically inspects and issues a list of approved colleges. These colleges meet the license requirements of various states in the United States and of most of the provinces of Canada. All CCE–approved chiropractic colleges offer a comprehensive course of study that prepares the student to pass licensing examinations and perform competently in the profession.

Chiropractic colleges that are accredited are recognized throughout the nation at both the federal and state levels. On the federal level, the U.S. Department of Education recognizes those colleges having status with the CCE and so lists them in its education directory. Certified chiropractic colleges are eligible for guaranteed student loans, student work-study programs, and interest assistance programs. Chiropractic is listed in the *Occupational Outlook Handbook* of the U.S. Department of Labor. Chiropractic colleges are eligible for loans from the U.S. Department of Housing and Urban Development. In addition, the Veterans Administration recognizes chiropractic institutions as institutions of higher education, and student visas for chiropractic students are granted by the U.S. Department of Immigration and Naturalization.

On the national level, a substantial number of accredited colleges in various states include a prechiropractic curriculum in their catalogs, and it is not uncommon to transfer credit from chiropractic colleges to regionally accredited institutions. Several chiropractic colleges have established cooperative programs with regionally accredited institutions of higher education.

Although most students attend chiropractic colleges in the United States, students may apply to foreign colleges. However, travel expenses and the lack of fellowships and scholarships may be a hindrance to some prospective students. College officials will weigh all applications against a number of factors, including grades in high school and in the two or more years of prechiropractic college training, and extracurricular activities that show evidence of the student's ability to get along with others.

International students must meet the same preprofessional academic criteria as American students. Furthermore, international students must have valid documents of admission to the United States. If any questions arise about the American equivalency of the student's international training, it is the responsibility of the student to obtain a letter of explanation and approval from the CCE.

Questions You May Wish to Ask a College

- *What are the educational principles of the program?* There are a variety of program styles and you will want to find one that best suits your leaning needs. Some colleges are more fundamental in their teaching style and others are more progressive, focusing on active learning methods in which the student takes part in the responsibility for learning and evaluation.
- *What is the college environment like?* Each college has a different mix of international students, minority groups, men/

women, religious backgrounds, and older students. The location of the college may also determine the types of students and patients that are seen in the clinical training program.

- *What types of chiropractic techniques are taught?* Some colleges teach a few core spinal techniques, while others have a broader perspective and include lower-impact techniques. Some colleges offer a variety of techniques either in the core curriculum or as elective courses.
- *When does active-technique skills training begin?* Chiropractic adjusting is a psychomotor skill. Some programs begin this training earlier, with the intention of assisting the students in mastering their adjusting skills.
- *Does the curriculum include adjunct or additional therapies?* Some colleges offer electives or continuing education classes in acupuncture, soft tissue treatments, and other alternative therapies.
- *How comprehensive is the library's collection of textbooks, videotapes, audiotapes, journals, and electronic resources?* Each college has a library that can be used as a learning resource. You may also want to ask if there are additional biomedical libraries nearby that will also add to the learning resources.
- *What are the college facilities like?* Many colleges have updated audiovisual technology to improve learning in the classroom as well as extensive computer labs. Some colleges are now integrating the use of laptop computers and Web-based programs to enhance the learning environment.
- *How busy are the college's clinics?* The clinics are where the active clinical training occurs; thus understanding the type of clinical training facilities will help you understand how clinical training occurs. Many colleges incorporate "outreach"

clinics as well as the core college clinic, where students may find more real-world office-practice experience. Clinics in low-income areas, affiliated with organizations such as the Salvation Army, and in integrated clinics and hospitals provide a variety of settings in which students learn the various primary settings for when they begin practice.

- *When does clinical training begin?* Some programs start the clinical experience early, so those students are exposed sooner to the clinical learning environment.
- *What type of practice-management skills courses are offered?* Each college has a slightly different approach in how to train its graduates for successful practice.
- *Are there programs to assist with job placement, practice-management skills, and clinic setup?* Some colleges offer classes on successful and ethical practice of chiropractic, and some offer educational and informational assistance with setting up practice during the year immediately following graduation.

Visiting Chiropractic Colleges

It is a good idea to visit your top three schools in person. This investment is modest compared to the tuition for the full educational period, and the information you gather is essential for your final decision. It is important to identify where you will be most productive during your educational experience, factoring in climate, educational and practice philosophies, size of the college, average age of the student body, and your other personal considerations.

All too often students select their college by location, personal recommendation, or simply the weather. It is incumbent upon the student to undertake the same due diligence in selecting a college as it is in selecting the career that he or she will ultimately choose for a lifetime.

When you visit chiropractic colleges, it is often helpful to make an appointment with a staff member of the admissions department. These staff members can organize campus tours, answer questions, introduce you to students and faculty members, and direct you toward resources for financial aid and housing. While you are visiting, be sure to ask the questions listed above and compare the answers that you receive from various colleges to see which one best suits your needs.

Chiropractic Colleges in North America

To increase chances of acceptance, students should apply to two or three colleges. The chiropractic colleges in North America are listed below. For more information and a list of other colleges around the world, see Appendix B.

Canadian Memorial Chiropractic College (Toronto)
Cleveland Chiropractic College (Kansas City, MO)
Cleveland Chiropractic College (Los Angeles)
D'Youville College (Buffalo, NY)
Life Chiropractic College West (Hayward, CA)
Life University College of Chiropractic (Marietta, GA)
Logan College of Chiropractic (Chesterfield, MO)
National University of Health Sciences (Lombard, IL)
New York Chiropractic College (Seneca Falls, NY)
Northwestern Health Sciences University
   (Bloomington, MN)
Palmer College of Chiropractic (Davenport, IA)

Palmer College of Chiropractic, Florida (Port Orange)
Palmer College of Chiropractic West (San Jose, CA)
Parker College of Chiropractic (Dallas, TX)
Sherman College of Straight Chiropractic
    (Spartanburg, SC)
Southern California University of Health Sciences
    (Whittier, CA)
Texas Chiropractic College (Pasadena, TX)
University of Bridgeport College of Chiropractic
    (Bridgeport, CT)
University of Quebec at Trois-Rivières (Montreal)
Western States Chiropractic College (Portland, OR)

To begin determining which of these colleges might be best for you, call or write them and ask for information to be sent to your home. You can review the information and begin formulating a list of your top schools.

6

The Chiropractic College Experience

Chiropractic colleges require a minimum of four academic years of professional resident study, including clinical experience under strict supervision, preceded by a minimum of two years of college work with a prescribed content. The first two years of professional study typically emphasize life sciences, health sciences, and clinical disciplines. The remaining two years typically emphasize practical or clinical studies dealing with the diagnosis and treatment of disease and other health-care issues, with approximately half the time comprised of training in the college clinics.

Profile of a Typical Chiropractic Student

The typical student body is made up of approximately three-fourths male, one-fourth female, twenty-four years of age. About half of the students are married and have an average of one child.

This typical student is a U.S. citizen; approximately 5 percent are foreign students.

Prior to entering chiropractic college, the student attended an accredited college and/or university during which time he or she completed a minimum of sixty to ninety semester hours of college credit, including a prescribed curriculum of biologic and physical science courses. Approximately 54 percent have bachelor's degrees, 21 percent have associate degrees, 2 percent have Ph.D. degrees, and 9 percent hold other degrees. Prior to selecting chiropractic as a career, many students were chiropractic patients and received information on chiropractic as a career from a doctor of chiropractic.

Student Orientation

During the first week of the academic year, most colleges conduct orientation sessions for first-year students as a means of introducing them to their new environment. These orientation sessions typically are mandatory and include discussions of the institution's objectives, organizational structure, procedures, scholastic regulations, student demeanor, student complaint procedures, requirements for successful completion of class work, class promotion, and requirements for graduation.

Emphasis is usually given to defining a student's position in relation to the profession, including an explanation of the legal, economic, and social place of the profession within society. In addition, students are given an understanding of state regulations of the profession and the role of the examining boards, as a protection for both the public and the practitioners licensed to practice.

Students are expected to present themselves as student doctors of chiropractic in both attitude and appearance. The educational process at a chiropractic college is designed not only to teach the technical skills necessary for successful practice, but also to develop the professional image and attitude of a health-care provider. To this end, students are expected to comply with standards of dress, appearance, and conduct established by the college, which are usually presented during orientation.

Curriculum

The purpose of the curriculum is to provide the means for giving a student a thorough understanding of the structure and function of the human organism in health and disease. A well-balanced presentation will give the student an understanding of the essential features of life processes in health and disease. Digestion, metabolism, excretion, physical and mental growth, nutrition, energy, nervous control, the significance of development defects, human behavior, and other elements are fundamental to the understanding of pathologic conditions. An understanding of structure and function makes it possible for students to identify deviations from the normal and provides the essential facts required in practice for diagnosis, treatment, or referral.

Several colleges utilize a variety of instructional strategies in addition to lectures and laboratory presentations. Problem-based methods, which emphasize self-directed learning, provide for integration of basic science information by use of clinical case studies. Standardized patients are also being utilized to evaluate clinical and interpersonal skills before entry into the patient-care setting.

The curriculum in a recognized chiropractic college is presented over a minimum period of eight semesters or the equivalent of a total of no fewer than forty-two hundred hours. This comprehensive course of instruction is presented in a proper sequence of subjects to ensure necessary prerequisites. Courses are taught in sufficient depth to fulfill the concept of the chiropractic physician as set forth within the educational standards of the Council on Chiropractic Education.

Doctor of Chiropractic degree programs include the following subjects (not necessarily in individual courses for each subject): anatomy; biochemistry; physiology; microbiology; pathology; public health; physical, clinical, and laboratory diagnosis; gynecology and obstetrics; pediatrics; geriatrics; dermatology; otolaryngology; diagnostic imaging procedures (radiology); psychology; nutrition/dietetics; biomechanics; orthopedics; neurology; first aid and emergency procedures; spinal analysis; principles and practice of chiropractic; clinical decision making; adjustive techniques; research methods and procedures; and professional practice ethics and other relevant courses. Each subject may appear as a standalone course in the curriculum or may be integrated throughout the program.

Basic science courses, such as anatomy and physiology, usually include laboratories where students conduct various experiments to understand how the human body works. In anatomy labs, several colleges now integrate computer software programs with the dissection of cadavers to provide multiple formats for learning this important topic.

Important aspects of learning to become a chiropractor include in-depth instruction in diagnostic and patient-care skills. Students learn how to use diagnostic equipment in clinical laboratory settings, where they can practice these skills to become proficient. Central to clinical education are courses that teach students how to thoroughly analyze the spine. In such courses, students learn in hands-on formats how to perform postural evaluation, spinal palpation, orthopedic and neurological tests, and other procedures commonly used in chiropractic practice.

There are usually several courses where students learn how to perform adjustments on the spine and upper and lower extremities. In these courses, students are taught how to appropriately use their hands to deliver highly skilled chiropractic adjustments. Other courses often teach students how to care for the soft tissues of the musculoskeletal system and perform various rehabilitation procedures and protocols.

Students typically progress from classroom learning to providing care for other chiropractic students under the direct supervision of clinical faculty members. When specific requirements are completed in this learning environment, students begin providing care for the public as chiropractic interns. Interns also practice under the supervision of clinical faculty.

For more information about each of the colleges' curricula, you should go to their individual websites listed in Appendix B or visit the Association of Chiropractic College's website (chirocolleges .org).

Academic Standing and Grading

In the typical chiropractic college, a grade of 70 percent is considered passing, but a cumulative average of 75 percent (2.0 GPA) or higher for the semester must be maintained to remain in good standing.

Every effort is made by the various instructors to assist students who are experiencing difficulty in mastering course materials. If it is determined that the student does not possess the aptitude and is unable to make satisfactory progress or is unwilling to cooperate with offered faculty assistance, the student will be advised to withdraw from the college.

Grading System

Grades are assigned on a typical academic scale. Some colleges use a plus and minus system.

When the majority of course work is completed, but a student is unable to finish an examination or assignment due to extenuating circumstances, an "incomplete" is usually assigned, and the student has the responsibility of completing all course work the following term. Some colleges do not consider a D grade to be a passing score, and students will need to retake the course and achieve a C grade or better to be given credit for the course. Additionally, several colleges issue a remediation (R) grade for some technical courses. A student may receive an R if he or she demonstrates proficiency in lecture material, but needs further skill development in laboratory material, such as chiropractic technique or diagnosis.

Failure of a subject requires that the course be repeated. If the course failure occurred due to failure of the final examination, a special repeat examination may be given with the approval of the instructor and the academic dean. The maximum possible grade on such an examination is usually 75. A charge is often required for this service.

Probation and Suspension

If a student's grade point average falls below 2.0, or should there be as many as two failures during any one semester, the student is placed on academic probation in the typical chiropractic college.

To be removed from probation, the student must earn a minimum grade point average of 2.0 for the next semester and must demonstrate a cumulative grade point average of 2.0.

A student beginning a semester on probation and failing to attain a 2.0 for that semester is usually subject to suspension. Should a student earn a grade point average below 1.0 for a semester, or fail three courses in a semester, the student is subject to suspension.

Students readmitted after suspension continue on probation and may be denied advanced standing until all deficiencies are satisfactorily corrected, unless given permission by the academic dean. A student is rarely readmitted after a second suspension.

Examinations

All students are expected to take all examinations during a term. If an examination is missed for a documented reason, a make-up examination may be given at the discretion of the instructor. For the second such make-up examination, a fee is usually required. Every effort should be made by the student to reach a mutually satisfactory arrangement with the instructor to take the examination within a given period of time following the date of the originally scheduled examination. In most instances, students will not be given the opportunity to make up more than two examinations in any one subject.

Failure of an examination does not necessarily entitle a student to repeat the exam. Final examinations are to be taken at the scheduled time unless special arrangements are made in advance with the instructor. Failure to take a final examination at the scheduled time usually subjects the student to a fee for any special final examinations administered.

Class Attendance

Regular and punctual attendance at all scheduled classes is expected of all students. A student may be dropped from a course or may receive a reduced or failing grade for excessive absences. Three incidences of tardiness in most chiropractic colleges may, at the discretion of the instructor, constitute an absence. Some states require a mandatory number of hours of participation in the classroom for the candidate to be licensed in that state. The colleges in those states require rigorous attendance records for all students.

Discipline

When a student is dropped from the rolls for absences, failing grades, or misconduct, he or she may apply for readmission at the beginning of the next semester. The administration reserves the right to dismiss any student at the request of the faculty, the ethics committee, or at its own discretion. There is no refund of tuition in the case of such a dismissal.

Student Services

Numerous services and opportunities exist for students at chiropractic colleges. These services aid students in successfully completing the academic program and transitioning into a chiropractic career.

Student Guidance and Counseling

The deans and faculty members in the chiropractic colleges make every effort to assist students with their problems and needs. Students are assigned to a faculty counselor and are encouraged to seek her or his assistance and guidance as necessary. In addition, administrative officers and consultants are available to help students with specific problems. Usually, these services may be accessed through the college department of student services.

College Libraries

Chiropractic college libraries provide a useful program of learning-resource services for students, faculty, research personnel, and the profession in general. The resources and acquisitions exist for the purpose of training health-care professionals and for developing a multimedia approach to augment and support the educational objectives. Thousands of scientific volumes and hundreds of scientific and professional journals are available to enhance the educational and research objectives of the college. Audiovisual aids, computers, and equipment for student and staff to use are available in the basic and clinical sciences.

College Laboratories

In the typical chiropractic college, laboratories are designed for teaching, research, and patient diagnosis. Laboratory instruction is provided in gross anatomy, biomechanics, physiology, pathology, microbiology, chemistry, chiropractic technique, histology, clinical laboratory diagnosis, physical diagnosis, physical therapy, and radiology. In addition, the college usually has one or more research laboratories for continuing research.

College Clinics

Each college has one or more outpatient clinics for training junior and senior interns. The facilities are equipped with a variety of standard and/or research-oriented analytic, diagnostic, and therapeutic equipment designed to offer modern health-care services. Office workspaces are available for both interns and staff doctors to meet to discuss patient care and management.

Student Benefits

Chiropractic health services are provided for all students in the outpatient clinic(s). Special rates are available for the families of married students.

As a member of certain student organizations, such as the SACA, students may be eligible to participate in professional group insurance at nominal fees.

Student Organizations

Student participation in organizational and group activities is of value in developing professional responsibility and attitudes. Through these activities, students become conditioned to their participation in the profession to support its colleges and its local, state, and national organizations for professional growth. For example, the Student American Chiropractic Association (SACA) is affiliated with the American Chiropractic Association. It gives each member a four-year start in becoming a part of the profession. It attempts to give each member a greater understanding of what is occurring in the profession on local, state, and national levels. Incorporated in this organization are representatives of each class, who act as members of a governing committee and council for student government.

Numerous student organizations and clubs are available on campus. State and national political organizations are present on every campus. Clubs focusing on chiropractic techniques, chiropractic specialties, public speaking, and community service are common.

Other special interest groups, including religious affiliations and ethnic backgrounds, are available. Students are encouraged to seek out the memberships that best suit their interests.

College Fraternities and Sororities

These social organizations are engaged in promoting good fellowship, social recreation, and professional responsibilities. They are frequently involved in charitable projects within the community, developing special educational programs and assisting the college to meet special goals. Membership is typically by invitation.

College Honorary Society

Membership in college honorary societies is open to those who maintain high academic standards. The purpose of these societies is to honor those students who have attained a high level of scholastic achievement. The obligations of its members are to exemplify the chiropractic image and aid those who need scholastic assistance.

College Athletic Clubs

The typical chiropractic college has a variety of athletic clubs, with faculty counseling and support, that arrange for participation in area-sponsored basketball, softball, and other athletic programs. Participation, based on sufficient student interest, is available in a variety of competitive activities such as bowling, golf, tennis, football, volleyball, soccer, hockey, rugby, and softball. Recreational facilities for a number of sports and recreational activities are usually available on campus.

The more the chiropractic student actively participates in athletic events, the more he or she will be able to appreciate human biomechanics and the causes and implications of athletic and recreational injuries. Students soon realize that amateur athletes and weekend recreation enthusiasts do not protect themselves against spinal problems as do professionals. Proper health counsel is best given when founded upon personal experience.

The National Board of Chiropractic Examiners

Students who wish to practice in the United States must pass several tests that are administered by the National Board of Chiropractic Examiners (NBCE). The NBCE is the principal testing agency for the chiropractic profession. It was established in 1963 after studies showed that exam scores from standardized national examinations, when developed and administered according to established testing industry guidelines, can provide certain benefits to a health-care profession.

In providing standardized academic and clinical testing services to the chiropractic profession, the NBCE develops, administers, analyzes, scores, and reports results from various examinations. The National Board test results are among the criteria utilized by state licensing agencies in determining whether applicants satisfy that state's minimum qualifications for licensure.

In its role as a national and international testing agency, the NBCE represents no particular chiropractic approach, philosophy, or college. The agency's examinations are formulated according to information provided collectively by the chiropractic colleges, the state licensing agencies, field practitioners, and subject specialists.

In developing National Board examinations, the NBCE staff utilizes the services of numerous chiropractic and educational consultants, as well as writers from throughout the profession, in preparing a comprehensive pool of test material. The tests are presented to committees typically composed of chiropractic educators and practitioners, subject specialists, and chiropractic members of state licensing boards. After several stages of careful review, the items deemed most viable by the committees appear on future examinations.

The examinations are administered at a total of eighteen test sites in the United States, Canada, England, France, and Australia. The NBCE examination content includes the following areas:

- **Part I.** A basic science subjects examination covering general anatomy, spinal anatomy, physiology, chemistry, pathology, microbiology, and public health. Students usually sit for this examination during the second academic year of chiropractic college, when they have completed all courses that are tested in Part I.
- **Part II.** A clinical-science subjects examination covering general diagnosis, neuromusculoskeletal diagnosis, diagnostic imaging, principles of chiropractic, chiropractic practice, and associated clinical sciences. Students usually sit for this examination during the third academic year of chiropractic college, when they have completed all courses that are tested in Part II.
- **Physiotherapy.** An elective examination assessing physical therapy modalities; their indications, contraindications, and applications; and therapeutic exercise and rehabilitation. Students sit for this examination once they have completed the courses pertaining to physiotherapy at their college, which is typically at the end of the second academic year or early part of the third academic year.
- **Part III.** A written clinical competency examination that addresses case history, physical examination, neuromusculoskeletal examination, roentgenologic examination, clinical laboratory and special studies, diagnosis or clinical impression, chiropractic technique, supportive techniques, and case management. Students usually sit for this examination during the fourth academic year of

chiropractic college, when they have completed all courses that are tested in Part III and are almost finished with clinical training.

• **Part IV.** This practical exam utilizes an Objective Structured Clinical Examination methodology and tests individuals in three major areas including x-ray interpretation and diagnosis, chiropractic technique, and case management. The Part IV examination may be taken when students are just about to graduate or just after they have graduated from chiropractic college.

• **SPEC.** The Special Purposes Examination for Chiropractic is designed specifically for utilization by state or foreign licensing agencies when considering cases of reciprocity/endorsement; reinstatement following licensure lapse, suspension, or revocation; and so forth. SPEC is designed to assess individuals who are licensed and have practiced two or more years. To establish eligibility to take SPEC, individuals must meet the following requirements: the applicant must hold a Doctor of Chiropractic degree from a chiropractic college whose students or graduates are eligible to take the NBCE exams; the applicant must be (or have been) licensed to practice chiropractic for at least two years prior to the published application receipt deadline; and the applicant must provide authorization from a state or international licensing agency. This authorization may be in the form of a requirement or request.

Following the administration of a National Board examination, scoring and analyses are facilitated by the use of various statistical programs. All programs are checked for accuracy and monitored at each stage of implementation.

Individual test items are scrutinized to determine how well they functioned under actual test conditions. NBCE test items must be relevant to chiropractic education and practice, and they must accurately reflect proficiency among examinees. Once final scores are calculated, the examinee and the colleges are notified. For more information about these examinations, you can visit the NBCE website (nbce.org).

Professional Degree and Licensure Requirements

Upon acceptable completion of the four-year college program, the degree of D.C. (Doctor of Chiropractic) is awarded. The candidate must have completed the prescribed curriculum of the college and have complied with all its regulations. Persons registered as special students who already hold a doctorate in chiropractic cannot be candidates for a duplicate degree.

To legally practice chiropractic, both a degree and the passing of licensure examinations must occur. In all states, the District of Columbia, Puerto Rico, and in most Canadian provinces, there are specific laws governing the practice of chiropractic and prescribing requirements for chiropractic licensure. These jurisdictions have examining boards that are usually composed of chiropractic physicians and laypeople. In a few states, there are composite boards of doctors of chiropractic and doctors of medicine. At the present time, most licensing jurisdictions recognize or utilize the certificate of the National Board of Chiropractic Examiners.

An increasing number of states require a four-year bachelor's degree for state licensure. These states include: Florida, Kansas, Maryland, Montana, New Mexico, North Carolina, Rhode Island, Tennessee, West Virginia, and Wisconsin.

For more information visit the Federation of Chiropractic Licensing Boards (fclb.org), and for specific statistics for each state see its statistics page (fclb.org/directory/statistics.pdf). For a list of all state licensing boards, see Appendix C.

All boards require completion of a four-year chiropractic college course at an accredited program leading to the Doctor of Chiropractic degree. For licensure, most state boards recognize either all or part of the four-part test administered by the National Board of Chiropractic Examiners. State examinations may supplement the National Board tests, such as examinations in state law and jurisprudence, depending on each state's requirements.

Continuing Education

Recognizing that any healing art must keep abreast of new data and procedures, the chiropractic profession supports continuing education as a mandatory yearly requirement for licensure in at least forty-seven of the fifty states. More states are supporting this effort each year. Appendix C provides a list of all state licensing boards, and their websites usually include continuing education information. Many states have also recognized the continuing education requirement for approximately twenty-four hours over two years, some of which may be obtained by self-study programs and distance learning.

This recognition has eased the financial burden upon the practitioner and permitted new and innovative programs to be delivered in an interactive fashion via Web-based learning. The wave of tomorrow's learning experience appears to be a movement toward interactive, personal-choice, Web-based contemporary programs. Although self-study Web-based programs are increasingly more popular, a part of the chiropractic profession's rich heritage is the graduate's continuation of longtime personal relationships that develop through personal attendance at conferences and seminars.

Each accredited chiropractic college maintains an ongoing postgraduate/continuing education department whose objective is to provide postgraduate education to better assist the doctor of chiropractic in the care of the public. Each postgraduate department produces programs, courses, and seminars that are designed to upgrade the competence, knowledge, and ability of graduate doctors of chiropractic. Many state associations offer continuing education programs as well.

7

Financing a Chiropractic Education

Before deciding to embark on a chiropractic career, a prospective student should investigate the financial commitment necessary to complete the education. Completing chiropractic college requires rigorous study and focus on the academic program. For this reason, many students take out student loans. Student loan debt can be minimized with a well-planned budget, conservative lifestyle, and by drawing upon part-time employment and scholarships.

Costs

In higher education generally, and in professional education particularly, the cost to the student is far less than the total educational cost involved. In chiropractic colleges, this difference is subsidized by the profession and by contributions from donors. Specific information on costs to the student will be found in the annual college catalog of each institution. When planning ahead, a good budget should incorporate some money for unexpected items.

Tuition

In general, a student today can expect tuition to run approximately $13,000 to $16,000 per academic year, where two semesters or three trimesters make up an academic year. Most programs are ten to eleven trimesters, or thirteen to fourteen quarters in length. Typically, $400 to $600 per semester is budgeted for miscellaneous fees and required supplies and books.

Equipment

When students enter clinical studies they will be required to purchase basic diagnostic instruments such as a stethoscope, otoscope, ophthalmoscope, blood pressure cuff (sphygmomanometer), and other items. The cost for a new and complete chiropractic doctor's diagnostic kit is $900 to $1,400. Slightly used diagnostic equipment can often be purchased at a reduced price; however, these usually do not include a manufacturer's warranty. The student should keep in mind that this equipment will be used throughout his or her future practice, so it's a good idea to invest in quality equipment, since it will be in service for a long time.

Living Expenses

Only a few chiropractic colleges have dormitories or apartments available to students. Living costs vary a great deal according to the tastes of the individual student and should account for the cost of living of the region in which the college is located. Living expenses including food and travel can range from $1,500 to $1,800 per month for a single student renting a room in a private home or sharing an apartment.

Student Scholarships

Various types of scholarships are available at all chiropractic colleges. The sources or the donors of scholarships vary as do the amount of each scholarship. State funds may also be available. Many states have commissions established for disbursement of funds to public and private nonprofit institutions for financial aid to eligible students.

There are several privately funded scholarships offered each year on a national basis through state chiropractic associations, auxiliary organizations, and fraternal organizations. In addition, each college has its private scholarship programs. Eligibility requirements are set by the sponsor of the scholarship. Generally, scholarships are awarded on the basis of academic achievement and financial need. For further information, contact the financial aid office of the college of your choice.

Many students can significantly reduce their student loan debt using scholarships, which is a good incentive for excellent academic performance. To be successful at receiving scholarships, students should check weekly with their financial aid office to find out immediately which scholarships are announced and when applications are due.

Student Financial Aid

In addition to scholarships, several forms of financial aid through loans and study-work programs are available at chiropractic colleges. These opportunities have become increasingly important as the costs of health education increase. The financial aid office should be contacted at each college for more details about specific loans, grants, and other funding opportunities.

All applicants for U.S. financial aid must be citizens of the United States, and applications for financial aid can be made only by those students who have been accepted by a specific college and have submitted the required entrance deposits. As financial aid funds must be distributed among those students actually enrolled, financial aid can only be awarded to those students who have reserved a position within the next term. After the entrance deposit has been received and a position has been held within classes, the necessary application forms will be forwarded to the student. This usually includes a financial need analysis form that must be completed.

Prospective students should keep in mind that financial aid offices at chiropractic colleges seek to help students with limited financial resources the best they can. However, as the amount of aid available through outside agencies is limited, it should be assumed that students will use their own resources (including scholarships and family contributions) to the fullest extent prior to applying for other forms of assistance. Only after these resources have been exhausted will a college be able to offer further assistance with funds over which it is custodian.

Student Loans

Most loans can be applied for through the Free Application for Federal Student Aid (FAFSA). The college's financial aid office uses this document to determine your need for all the available aid, such as the Federal Perkins and Federal Stafford Loan programs. The student can complete the FAFSA online (fafsa.ed.gov) or with a paper application. If the chiropractic college code is submitted electronically, the college will receive the form electronically, thus speeding up this process. Eligibility for financial assistance involving federal funds is based primarily upon the student's demonstrated need.

Federal Perkins Loan

The Federal Perkins Loan (formerly National Direct Student Loan) is a 5 percent interest loan. Interest does not begin to accrue until repayment starts. Repayment generally begins nine months after you leave school. The advantages of this loan include low interest rates and generously extended repayment periods. The loan limit varies per year but is about $1,000 per quarter. Each college is authorized a certain amount of money each year to distribute among eligible students. To be eligible, students must show need and ability to maintain acceptable academic standing.

Subsidized Stafford Loan Program

Under the provisions of this program, a student may obtain low interest educational loans with repayment deferred until after the student completes his or her education. The loan limit for an independent graduate or professional student is about $8,500 per academic year, in addition to the limits imposed by the Unsubsidized Stafford Loan, whose description follows. A combined origination/insurance fee of 3 percent is automatically deducted from each loan disbursement. For this loan, as long as the borrower is in school at least half-time, the federal government pays the interest while the student is in school and through the six-month grace period. The student should allow four to six weeks for application processing.

Unsubsidized Stafford Loan Program

The loan limit for a student is approximately $22,500 per academic year in addition to the Subsidized Stafford Loan limits. A combined origination/insurance fee of 3 percent is automatically deducted from each loan disbursement. The interest begins to accrue immediately as soon as the loan is approved, while you are in school and during repayment for this loan.

ChiroLoan

The credit-based ChiroLoan may be used to supplement other forms of financial assistance. You may borrow $1,000 to $10,000 annually, provided you have an unmet need and a satisfactory personal credit history. The interest rate is variable and is based on the 91-day Treasury Bill yield plus 2.5 percent while you are in school, and on the 91-day Treasury Bill yield plus 2.9 percent when you begin repayment. A 10 percent guarantee fee is deducted from the loan check when the loan is disbursed.

Canadian ChiroLoan

The credit-based Canadian ChiroLoan may be used to supplement other forms of financial assistance. Canadian students who have a satisfactory personal credit history may borrow up to $15,000 annually. The interest rate is variable and is based on the 91-day Treasury Bill yield plus 2.5 percent while you are in school, and on the 91-day Treasury Bill yield plus 2.9 percent when you begin repayment. A 10 percent guarantee fee is deducted from the loan check when the loan is disbursed.

Student Work-Study Programs

Two different work-study programs are available on most campuses. Work-study is an excellent way to earn money while learning more about chiropractic.

Federal Work-Study Program (FWSP)

This is a campus-based work program, funded jointly by the college and the federal government, that provides jobs on campus for students who work five to a maximum of twenty hours each week at an hourly rate for students determined by the position. Students must be enrolled at least half-time to qualify under this program. The institution provides available positions for students in areas such as library, audiovisual aids, business office, admissions, clerical work, building maintenance, research, and laboratory assistance. As the support funds received from the Department of Education are limited, a student must demonstrate need as shown by a financial need analysis. This program can also be applied to through FAFSA.

College Supported Work-Study

Some opportunities for work-study exist on campuses outside of the federal program. While funds for such programs are usually limited because they come directly from the college's operating budget, students should check to see if any are available if they do not qualify for federal work study. This may be particularly important for foreign students, or students taking loans from private sources such as family.

Part-Time Employment

Many students find it necessary to supplement their financial income by part-time work while attending chiropractic college. About half of the students attending chiropractic colleges engage in part-time work with or without the assistance of their schools.

However, the curriculum demands the major portion of the student's time and energy. Therefore, it is not wise for a student to attempt to earn her or his entire college and living expenses, while at the same time trying to follow the required course of study.

Students are encouraged to stay away from graveyard shifts, late-night jobs, and extensive workloads because they typically find that the round-the-clock lifestyle quickly exhausts them. Exhaustion leads to declining academic performance and illness, and students should well avoid this situation. Students who decide to work part-time should consider their job options carefully. Securing a part-time job in a chiropractor's office may be a good choice, because it can be both financially beneficial and educational at the same time.

Appendix A

Chiropractic Organizations and Websites

The Academy of Forensic and Industrial Chiropractic
   Consultants (AFICC), aficc.tripod.com
American Board of Chiropractic Internists,
   rollanet.org/~internis/dabci
American Board of Chiropractic Orthopedists,
   abconet.org
American Chiropractic Association, acatoday.com
American Chiropractic Association Sports Council,
   acasc.org
American Chiropractic Association's Council on
   Occupational Health, acacoh.com
American Chiropractic Board of Radiologists, acbr.org
American Chiropractic Board of Sports Physicians,
   acbsp.com
American Chiropractic College of Radiology, accr.org or
   dacbr.com
American Chiropractic Neurology Board, acnb.org
American Chiropractic Rehabilitation Board, acrb.org

American College of Chiropractic Consultants,
accc-chiro.com

American College of Chiropractic Orthopedists,
accoweb.org

American Public Health Association, Chiropractic Health
Care Section, c3r.org/chirohealth

Association of Chiropractic Colleges, chirocolleges.org

Association for the History of Chiropractic,
chirohistory.org

Canadian Chiropractic Association, ccachiro.org

Canadian Chiropractic Examining Board, cceb.ca

Chiropractic Educational Network, cenedu.com

The Chiropractic Report, chiropracticreport.com

Christian Chiropractic Association,
christianchiropractors.org

Congress of Chiropractic State Associations, cocsa.org

Council on Applied Chiropractic Sciences (CACS),
chiropractic.org/councils/cacs.htm

Council on Chiropractic Education (CCE), cce-usa.org

Council on Fitness and Sports Health Science,
chiropractic.org/councils/fitness.htm

Councils on Chiropractic Education International (CCEI),
cceintl.org

Dynamic Chiropractic, chiroweb.com

European Chiropractors' Union, chiropractic-ecu.org

Federation of Chiropractic Licensing Boards, fclb.org

Foundation for Chiropractic Education and Research,
fcer.org

ICA Council on Chiropractic Pediatrics,
chiropractic.org/councils/pediatrics.htm

International Academy of Chiropractic Neurology,
   iacn.com
The International Academy of Olympic Chiropractic
   Officers, iaoco.org
International Chiropractors' Association, chiropractic.org
International Federation of Sports Chiropractic/Federation
   Internationale de Chiropratique du Sport (FICS),
   fics-online.org
National Board of Chiropractic Examiners, nbce.org
National Board of Forensic Chiropractors,
   forensicexaminers.org
Texas Back Institute, texasback.com
World Federation of Chiropractic, wfc.org

Doctor of Chiropractic Programs

THIS APPENDIX LISTS accredited colleges of chiropractic in the United States, Australia, Canada, United Kingdom, France, Denmark, Brazil, Korea, New Zealand, Japan, and South Africa.

Doctor of Chiropractic Programs in the United States

Cleveland Chiropractic College, Kansas City
6401 Rockhill Rd.
Kansas City, MO 64131
clevelandchiropractic.edu
Continuously accredited since June 1982

Cleveland Chiropractic College, Los Angeles
590 N. Vermont Ave.
Los Angeles, CA 90004
clevelandchiropractic.edu
Continuously accredited since January 1985

D'Youville College
One D'Youville Square
320 Porter Ave.
Buffalo, NY 14201
dyc.edu
See cce-usa.org for current accreditation status.

Life Chiropractic College West
25001 Industrial Blvd.
Hayward, CA 94545
lifewest.edu
Continuously accredited since July 1987

Life University College of Chiropractic
1269 Barclay Circle
Marietta, GA 30060
life.edu
See cce-usa.org for current accreditation status.

Logan College of Chiropractic
P.O. Box 1065
Chesterfield, MO 63006-1065
logan.edu
Continuously accredited since June 1978

Los Angeles College of Chiropractic
The Southern California University of Health Sciences
P.O. Box 1166
Whittier, CA 90609-1166
scuhs.edu
Continuously accredited since January 1971

National University of Health Sciences
College of Professional Studies
200 E. Roosevelt Rd.
Lombard, IL 60148-4583
nuhs.edu
Continuously accredited since January 1971

New York Chiropractic College
P.O. Box 800
Seneca Falls, NY 13148-0800
nycc.edu
Continuously accredited since January 1979

Northwestern College of Chiropractic
Northwestern Health Sciences University
2501 W. Eighty-fourth St.
Bloomington, MN 55431
nwhealth.edu
Continuously accredited since January 1971

Palmer College of Chiropractic
1000 Brady St.
Davenport, IA 52803
palmer.edu
Continuously accredited since July 1979

Palmer College of Chiropractic, Florida
4705 S. Clyde Morris Blvd.
Port Orange, FL 32129-4103
palmer.edu
Applying for CCE accreditation as of 2002

Palmer College of Chiropractic, West
90 E. Tasman Dr.
San Jose, CA 95134
palmer.edu
Continuously accredited since June 1985

Parker College of Chiropractic
2500 Walnut Hill La., Ste. 100E
Dallas, TX 75229-5668
parkercc.edu
Continuously accredited since June 1988

Sherman College of Straight Chiropractic
P.O. Box 1452
Spartanburg, SC 29304
sherman.edu
Continuously accredited since January 1995

Texas Chiropractic College
5912 Spencer Highway
Pasadena, TX 77505-1699
txchiro.edu
Continuously accredited since January 1971

University of Bridgeport College of Chiropractic
75 Linden Ave.
Bridgeport, CT 06601
bridgeport.edu/chiro
Continuously accredited since June 1994

Western States Chiropractic College
2900 NE 132nd Ave.
Portland, OR 97230
wschiro.edu
Continuously accredited since January 1981

Doctor of Chiropractic Programs Accredited by ACCE as of 2003

Macquarie University
Bldg. E7A, Ste. 222
Macquarie University NSW 2109
Australia
chiro.mq.edu.au

Royal Melbourne Institute of Technology
Department of Complementary Medicine
P.O. Box 71
Bundoora, Victoria 3083
Australia
rmit.edu.au/compmed

Doctor of Chiropractic Programs Accredited by CCE of Canada

Canadian Memorial Chiropractic College
1900 Bayview Ave.
Toronto, Ontario
Canada M4G 3E6
cmcc.ca

University of Quebec at Trois-Rivières
Module de Chiropratique
Universite du Quebec à Trois-Rivières
C.P. 500, Trois-Rivières, Quebec
Canada G9A 5H7
uqtr.ca/chiro

Doctor of Chiropractic Programs Accredited by European CCE

Anglo-European College of Chiropractic
13-15 Parkwood Rd., Bournemouth
Dorset, BH5 2DF
England
aecc.ac.uk

Institut Franco-Européen De Chiropratique
24 Avenue Paul Vaillant-Couturier
94200 Ivry-Sur-Seine
France
ifec.net

Syddansk Universitet Odense
Programme in Clinical Biomechanics
DK 5230 Odense M
Denmark
sdu.dk

University of Glamorgan
School of Applied Sciences, B.Sc. Honours Chiropractic
Pontypridd, Mid Glamorgan CF37 1DL
Wales
glam.ac.uk

Other Chiropractic Colleges

Hanseo University, RMIT Unit
136-220 Jaegi-2 Dong Dongdaemoon-Ku
Seoul, Korea
E-mail: chiropia@hotmail.com

Aspeur/Feevale
Rua Emillo Hauschild
70-Villa Nova
Caixa postal 2121
Novo Hamburgo
RS-CEP 93525.180
Brazil
Phone: 55-51-594-2122
Fax: 55-51-594-7977

New Zealand College of Chiropractic
P.O. Box 113-044
Newmarket, Auckland
New Zealand
chiropractic.ac.nz

RMIT University Chiropractic Unit, Japan
IK Bldg. 6-20-11, Shinbashi
Minato-ku, Tokyo 105-0004
Japan
chiro.co.jp/rmit-univ/english.htm

Technikon Natal
Nattechnikon 6-20187
953 Durban 4000
South Africa
ntech.ac.za

Technikon Witwatersrand
P.O. Box 17011
Doorntonetein 2028, JHB
South Africa
twr.ac.za

State Boards of Chiropractic Examiners

Alabama State Board of Chiropractic Examiners
737 Logan Rd.
Clanton, AL 35045
chiro.state.al.us

Alaska State Board of Chiropractic Examiners
Division of Occupational Licensing
333 Willoughby Ave., 9th Fl.
P.O. Box 110806
Juneau, AK 99811-0806
dced.state.ak.us/occ/pchi.htm

State of Arizona Board of Chiropractic Examiners
5060 N. Nineteenth Ave., Ste. 416
Phoenix, AZ 85015
azchiroboard.com

Arkansas State Board of Chiropractic Examiners
101 E. Capitol St., Ste. 209
Little Rock, AR 72201
state.ar.us/asbce

California Board of Chiropractic Examiners
2525 Natomas Park Dr., Ste. 260
Sacramento, CA 95833-2931
chiro.ca.gov

Colorado State Board of Chiropractic Examiners
1560 Broadway, Ste. 1310
Denver, CO 80202
dora.state.co.us/chiropractic

Connecticut State Board of Chiropractic Examiners
Chiropractic Licensure, Department of Public Health
410 Capitol Ave., MS# 12APP
P.O. Box 340308
Hartford, CT 06134
state.ct.us/dph

Delaware Board of Chiropractic
Cannon Bldg., Ste. 203
861 Silver Lake Blvd.
Dover, DE 19904
professionallicensing.state.de.us/boards/chiropractic/index.shtml

Government of the District of Columbia Board of Chiropractic
825 N. Capitol St. NE, 2nd Fl.
Washington, DC 20002-4210
asisvcs.com

Florida Board of Chiropractic Medicine
Department of Health
4052 Bald Cypress Way, Bin #C07
Tallahassee, FL 32399-3257
doh.state.fl.us/mqa/chiro/chiro_home.html

Georgia Board of Chiropractic Examiners
237 Coliseum Dr.
Macon, GA 31217
sos.state.ga.us/plb/chiro

Hawaii State Board of Chiropractic Examiners
Department of Commerce and Consumer Affairs
1010 Richards St.
Honolulu, HI 96813
state.hi.us/dcca/pvl

Idaho State Board of Chiropractic Physicians
1109 Main St., Ste. 220
Boise, ID 83702-5642
state.id.us/ibol/chi.htm

Illinois Medical Licensing Board
Medical Licensing Unit
Department of Professional Regulation
320 W. Washington, 3rd Fl.
Springfield, IL 62786
dpr.state.il.us

Indiana Board of Chiropractic Examiners
Health Professions Bureau
402 W. Washington St., Rm. 041
Indianapolis, IN 46204
in.gov/hpb/boards/ibce

Iowa Board of Chiropractic Examiners
Department of Public Health
Lucas State Office Building, 4th Fl.
321 E. Twelfth St.
Des Moines, IA 50319-0075
idph.state.ia.us

Kansas State Board of Healing Arts
235 S. Topeka Blvd.
Topeka, KS 66603
ksbha.org

Kentucky State Board of Chiropractic Examiners
P.O. Box 183
Glasgow, KY 42142-0183

Louisiana State Board of Chiropractic Examiners
8621 Summa Ave.
Baton Rouge, LA 70809
lachiropracticboard.com

Maine Board of Chiropractic Licensure
Department of Professional and Financial Regulation
35 State House Station
Augusta, ME 04333
maineprofessionalreg.org

Maryland Board of Chiropractic Examiners
Department of Health and Mental Hygiene
4201 Patterson Ave.
Baltimore, MD 21215-2299
mdchiro.org

Massachusetts Board of Registration of Chiropractors
239 Causeway St.
Boston, MA 02114
state.ma.us/reg/boards/ch

Michigan Board of Chiropractic
611 W. Ottawa
Lansing, MI 48933
P.O. Box 30670
Lansing, MI 48909
cis.state.mi.us/bhser

Minnesota Board of Chiropractic Examiners
2829 University Ave. SE, #300
Minneapolis, MN 55414-3220
mn-chiroboard.state.mn.us

Mississippi State Board of Chiropractic Examiners
P.O. Box 775
Louisville, MS 39339

Missouri State
3605 Missouri Blvd.
Jefferson City, MO 65109
P.O. Box 672
Jefferson City, MO 65102-0672
ecodev.state.mo.us/pr/chiro

Montana Board of Chiropractors
P.O. Box 200513
Helena, MT 59620-0513
discoveringmontana.com/dli/bsd

Board of Examiners in Chiropractic
Nebraska Health and Human Services
301 Centennial Mall S
P.O. Box 94986
Lincoln, NE 68509-4986
hhs.state.ne.us

Chiropractic Physicians' Board of Nevada
4600 Kietzke La., Ste. M-245
Reno, NV 89502
state.nv.us/chirobd

New Hampshire Board of Chiropractic Examiners
Health and Welfare Bldg.
6 Hazen Dr.
Concord, NH 03301-6527

New Jersey State Board of Chiropractic Examiners
124 Halsey St.
P.O. Box 45004
Newark, NJ 07101
state.nj.us/lps/ca/medical.htm

New Mexico Board of Chiropractic Examiners
2055 S. Pacheco, Ste. 400
P.O. Box 25101
Santa Fe, NM 87504

New York State Board for Chiropractic
89 Washington Ave., 2nd Fl.
Albany, NY 12234
op.nysed.gov

North Carolina Board of Chiropractic Examiners
174 N. Church St.
Concord, NC 28025
ncchiroboard.org

North Dakota State Board of Chiropractic Examiners
Highway 17W
P.O. Box 185
Grafton, ND 58237
governor.state.nd.us/boards/boards-query.asp?board_id=22

Ohio State Chiropractic Board
77 S. High St., 16th Fl.
Columbus, OH 43215
state.oh.us/chr

Oklahoma Board of Chiropractic Examiners
201 NE Thirty-eighth Terrace, Ste. 3
Oklahoma City, OK 73105
okchiropracticboard.com

Oregon Board of Chiropractic Examiners
3218 Pringle Rd. SE, Ste. 150
Salem, OR 97302-6311
obce.state.or.us

Pennsylvania State Board of Chiropractic
116 Pine St., 5th Fl.
P.O. Box 2649
Harrisburg, PA 17105-2649
dos.state.pa.us/bpoa/chibd/mainpage.htm

Puerto Rico, Junta Examinadora De Quiropracticos De Puerto Rico
P.O. Box 10200
Santurce, PR 00907

Rhode Island Board of Examiners in Chiropractic
Three Capitol Hill, Rm. 104
Providence, RI 02908-5097
fclb.org/directory/rhodeisland

South Carolina Board of Chiropractic Examiners
110 Centerview Dr., Ste. 306
Columbia, SC 29210
llr.state.sc.us/pol/chiropractors

South Dakota Board of Chiropractic Examiners
2603 Ella La.
Yankton, SD 57078
state.sd.us/dcr/chiropractic

Tennessee Board of Chiropractic Examiners
425 Fifth Ave. N, 1st Fl.
Cordell Hull Bldg.
Nashville, TN 37247-1010
state.tn.us/health

Texas Board of Chiropractic Examiners
333 Guadalupe, Tower III, Ste. 825
Austin, TX 78701
tbce.state.tx.us

Utah Chiropractic Physicians Licensing Board
160 E. 300 S
P.O. Box 146741
Salt Lake City, UT 84114-6741
commerce.state.ut.us

Vermont Board of Chiropractic
26 Terrace St., Drawer 09
Montpelier, VT 05609-1106
vtprofessionals.org/chiropractors

U.S. Virgin Islands Board of Chiropractic Examiners
Office of the Commissioner
48 Sugar Estate
St. Thomas, VI 00802

Virginia Board of Medicine, Dept. of Health Professions
6606 W. Broad St., 4th Fl.
Richmond, VA 23230
dhp.state.va.us

Washington Chiropractic Quality Assurance Commission
1300 SE Quince St.
P.O. Box 47867
Olympia, WA 98504-7867
doh.wa.gov/hsqa/hpqad/chiropractic/default.htm

West Virginia Board of Chiropractic Examiners
415½ D St., Ste. #6
P.O. Box 8532
South Charleston, WV 25303
state.wv.us/wvboc

Wisconsin Chiropractic Examining Board
1400 E. Washington Ave.
P.O. Box 8935
Madison, WI 53708
drl.state.wi.us

Wyoming State Board of Chiropractic Examiners
2020 Carey Ave., Ste. 201
Cheyenne, WY 82002
soswy.state.wy.us/director/ag-bd/chiro.htm

Bibliography

Bronfort, Gert, William J. J. Assendelft, Roni Evans, Mitchell Haas, and Lex Bouter. "Efficacy of Spinal Manipulation for Chronic Headache: A Systematic Review," *Journal of Manipulative and Physiological Therapeutics* 24 (2001): 457–66.

Cherkin, Daniel C., and F. A. MacCornack. "Patient Evaluations of Low Back Pain Care from Family Physicians and Chiropractors," *Western Journal of Medicine* 150 (1989): 351–55.

Christensen, Mark G., Darla Kerkoff, and Martin W. Kollach. *Job Analysis of Chiropractic, 2000: A Project Report, Survey Analysis, and Summary of Chiropractic Practice in the United States*. Greeley, Colo.: National Board of Chiropractic Examiners, 2000.

Coulter, Ian D. *Chiropractic: A Philosophy of Alternative Health Care*. Oxford: Butterworth-Heinemann, 1999.

Coulter, Ian D., Eric L. Hurwitz, Alan H. Adams, William C.
    Meeker, Dan T. Hansen, Ronert D. Mootz, Peter D. Aker,
    Barbara J. Genovese, and Paul G. Shekelle. *The
    Appropriateness of Manipulation and Mobilization of the
    Cervical Spine.* Santa Monica: RAND Corporation, 1996.
Curtis, P., and Geoffrey Bove. "Family Physicians, Chiropractors,
    and Back Pain," *Journal of Family Practice* 35 (1992): 551–55.
Eisenberg, David M., Roger B. Davis, Susan L. Ettner, Scott
    Appel, Sonja Wilkey, Maria Van Rompay, and Ronald C.
    Kessler. "Trends in Alternative Medicine Use in the United
    States, 1990–1997: Results of a Follow-Up National Survey,"
    Journal of the American Medical Association 280 (1998):
    1569–75.
Evans, Roni, Gert Bronfort, B. Nelson, and C. H. Goldsmith.
    "Two-Year Follow-Up of a Randomized Clinical Trial of
    Spinal Manipulation and Two Types of Exercises for Patients
    with Chronic Neck Pain," *Spine* 27 (2002): 2383–89.
Hurwitz, Eric L., Peter D. Aker, Alan H. Adams, William C.
    Meeker, and Paul G. Shekelle. "Manipulation and
    Mobilization of the Cervical Spine: A Systematic Review of
    the Literature," *Spine* 21 (1996): 1746–60.
Keating, Joseph C., Alana Callender, and Carl S. Cleveland III. *A
    History of Chiropractic Education in North America.*
    Davenport, Iowa: Association for the History of Chiropractic,
    1998.
Keating, Joseph. *B.J. of Davenport: The Early Years of Chiropractic.*
    Davenport, Iowa: Association for the History of Chiropractic,
    1997.
Korthals-de Bos, Ingeborg, Jan L. Hoving, Maurits W. van Tulder,
    Maureen P. M. H. Rutten-van Molken, Herman J. Ader,

Henrica C. W. de Vet, Bart W. Koes, Hindrik Vondeling, and Lex M. Bouter. "Cost Effectiveness of Physiotherapy, Manual Therapy, and General Practitioner Care for Neck Pain: Economic Evaluation Alongside a Randomised Controlled Trial," *British Medical Journal* 326 (2003): 911.

Manga, Pran, Douglas E. Angus, Costa Papadopoulos, and William R. Swan. *The Effectiveness and Cost-Effectiveness of Chiropractic Management of Low Back Pain.* Richmond Hill, Ontario: Kenilworth Publishing, 1993.

Maynard, Joseph. *Healing Hands: The Story of the Palmer Family and Developers of Chiropractic.* Woodstock, Ga: Jonorum Publishers, 1991.

Meade, Thomas W., S. Dyer, W. Browne, J. Townsend, and A. O. Frank. "Low Back Pain of Mechanical Origin: Randomised Comparison of Chiropractic and Hospital Outpatient Treatment," *British Medical Journal* 300 (1990): 1431–37.

Meeker, William C., and Scott Haldeman. "Chiropractic: A Profession at the Crossroads of Mainstream and Alternative Medicine," *Annals of Internal Medicine* 136 (2002): 216–27.

North American Spine Society. "Common Diagnostic and Therapeutic Procedures of the Lumbosacral Spine, the North American Spine Society's Ad-Hoc Committee on Diagnostic and Therapeutic Procedures," *Spine* 16 (1991): 1161–67.

Peterson, Dennis, and Glenda Wiese. *Chiropractic: An Illustrated History.* St. Louis: Mosby Year Book, Inc., 1995.

RAND. "Chiropractic Patients in a Comprehensive Home-Based Geriatric Assessment, Follow-Up, and Health Promotion Program," 1995.

Rupert, Ronald L. "A Survey of Practice Patterns and the Health Promotion and Prevention Attitudes of U.S. Chiropractors.

Maintenance Care: Part I," *Journal of Manipulative and Physiological Therapeutics* 23 (2000): 1–9.

Rupert, Ronald L., Donna Manello, and Ruth Sandefur. "Maintenance Care: Health Promotion Services Administered to U.S. Chiropractic Patients Aged 65 and Older, Part II," *Journal of Manipulative and Physiological Therapeutics* 23 (2000): 10–19.

Terrett, Allan G. J. "Misuse of the Literature by Medical Authors in Discussing Spinal Manipulative Therapy Injury," *Journal of Manipulative and Physiological Therapeutics* 18 (1995): 203–10.

Wardwell, Walter I. *Chiropractic: History and Evolution of a New Profession*. St. Louis: Mosby Year Book, Inc., 1992.

Wilk et al. v. AMA et al., 671 F. Supp. 1465, affirmed 895 F2d 352 (7th Cir 1990).

Wolsko, P. M., D. M. Eisenberg, R. B. Davis, R. Kessler, and R. S. Phillips. "Patterns and Perceptions of Care for Treatment of Back and Neck Pain: Results of a National Survey," *Spine* 28 (2003): 292–97.

About the Authors

Bart Green, D.C., M.S.Ed., received his chiropractic degree from the Los Angeles College of Chiropractic and his master's degree in health professions education from the University of Southern California, Keck School of Medicine. He also earned a diplomate from the American Chiropractic Board of Sports Physicians. He served as an associate professor and Associate Dean of Curriculum at Palmer College of Chiropractic West. Currently, he is a contracted chiropractic physician at Naval Medical Center, San Diego.

Dr. Green is an active chiropractic scholar, having published several scientific and educational articles in peer-reviewed journals. He serves as associate editor for the journal *Chiropractic History* and a research newsletter called the *Chiropractic Research Review* and has served as the editor for the *Journal of Sports Chiropractic and Rehabilitation*. He currently performs editorial review and peer review for several journals, including the *Journal of the Canadian Chiropractic Association*, *Journal of Manipulative and Physiological Therapeutics*, *Journal of Allied Health*, and *Medical Education Online*.

Dr. Green enjoys mentoring others to publish scholarly works, including doctors in master's programs, chiropractors in the field, fellow faculty members, and students. He enjoys providing a fresh and enthusiastic approach to the content that he teaches by trying to turn learning into a fun and rewarding experience.

Claire Johnson, D.C., M.S.Ed., is an associate clinical professor in the Departments of Research, Diagnosis, and Clinics at Palmer College of Chiropractic West (PCCW) and previously served as a faculty member at the Los Angeles College of Chiropractic. She is currently the Associate Dean of Student and Program Assessment at PCCW. She graduated from the Los Angeles College of Chiropractic in 1991, received her diplomate from the American Chiropractic Board of Sports Physicians in 1998, and earned a master's degree in Health Professions Education from the University of Southern California, Keck School of Medicine in 2000.

She has served as the Conference Chair and Peer Review Chair for the Association of Chiropractic Colleges (ACC) for the past six years and has focused on elevating the quality of clinical and basic science research presentations and the amount of educational research produced in chiropractic. Dr. Johnson recently coordinated the ACC Educational Conference 2003, as well as the Association for the History of Chiropractic Conference 2001. She serves as an editor for the clinician-oriented *Chiropractic Research Review* and is the former editor for the *Journal of Sports Chiropractic and Rehabilitation*. She currently serves on editorial review boards for *Medical Education Online* and the journals *Chiropractic History*, *Integrative Medicine*, and the *Journal of the Canadian Chiropractic Association*.

Dr. Johnson has published papers in journals such as *Topics in Clinical Chiropractic*, *Chiropractic History*, and the *Journal of*

Manipulative and Physiological Therapeutics. Her interests and experience are in the areas of clinical, educational, and historical research. She is known for her mentoring relationships that assist students and clinicians on their paths to publication and scholarly activities.

Louis Sportelli, D.C., is author of a patient education book entitled *Introduction to Chiropractic,* which is currently in its tenth edition. Several million of these books are in use throughout the world for public information on chiropractic. He has lectured extensively throughout the United States and has authored numerous articles for publication dealing with patient management, ethics, radiation protection, public relations, jurisprudence, and risk management, as well as health-care reform. He has also developed and designed anatomical charts for patient education on such topics as whiplash and osteoarthritis.

Dr. Sportelli has co-authored several texts: *Risk Management in Chiropractic, Medical-Legal Issues,* and *Chiropractic Form and Sample Letter Book.* He has served on the Board of Governors of the American Chiropractic Association from 1980 through 1989, serving as board chairman his last year.

Dr. Sportelli has been president of the National Chiropractic Mutual Insurance Holding Company since 1995. Among his honors is a fellowship in the Palmer Academy of Chiropractic Honorous Causa (1984), an honorary Doctor of Humanities degree from the Los Angeles College of Chiropractic (1986), and an honorary Doctor of Laws degree from the National College of Chiropractic (1988). He serves on the postgraduate faculty of the National College of Chiropractic. Dr. Sportelli has been in continuous practice in Palmerton, Pennsylvania, since 1962. He is married and has two daughters.